Promoting Meaningful Learning

Innovations in Educating Early Childhood Professionals

Nicola J. Yelland, Editor

A 2000 NAEYC Comprehensive Membership Benefit

National Association for the Education of Young Children
Washington, D.C.

National Association for the Education of Young Children
1509 16th Street, NW
Washington, DC 20036-1426
202-232-8777 or 800-424-2460
www.naeyc.org

Through its publications program the National Association for the Education of Young Children (NAEYC) provides a forum for discussion of major issues and ideas in the early childhood field, with the hope of provoking thought and promoting professional growth. The views expressed or implied are not necessarily those of the Association. NAEYC thanks the editor and contributors, who donated much time and effort to develop this book for the profession.

Library of Congress Card Number: 00-107974
ISBN 0-935989-96-X
NAEYC #138

Publications editor: Carol Copple
Production manager: Jack Zibulsky
Copy editors: Brian Baker and Catherine Cauman
Managing editor: Lacy Thompson
Editorial assistance: Natalie Klein
Cover design: Sandi Collins
Book design & production: Malini Dominey

Printed in the United States of America

For Gerald

Hos successus alit: possunt, quia posse videntur
—Virgil, *Aeneid*

(These successes encourage: they can because they think they can.)

Thanks are due to all the educators, parents, children, and community
groups who have supported us in the creation of this book.
Thanks also to our families who support us
in everything we do.

About the Contributors

Editor

Nicola J. Yelland teaches in the School of Early Childhood at Queensland University of Technology in Brisbane, Australia. She is a researcher in the Centre for Mathematics and Science Education and a Department of Education Training and Youth Affairs research fellow. Her current research is funded by the Australian Research Council and focuses on young children's learning in technological environments. She has published two books: *Gender in Early Childhood* and *Early Mathematical Explorations* with Carmel Diezmann and Deborah Butler.

Contributors

Cynthia à Beckett is a senior lecturer in early childhood education at the University of New England in Armidale, New South Wales, Australia. She was lecturer for many years in the School of Early Childhood at Queensland University of Technology, where she researched the material for her chapter. As a preschool adviser, she has researched and published in the arts, children's television, and the sociology of young children and families.

Anna Bower has a background as a practitioner and researcher in early special education. Her main areas of interest are families who have a child with a disability and the relationships between professionals and those families. Anna is an honorary associate researcher at the Fred and Eleanor Schonell Special Education Research Centre at the University of Queensland in Brisbane Australia.

Jenny Cartmel is an early childhood educator in Brisbane, who has worked with children, parents, and students in a diverse range of contexts, from preschool to tertiary institutions. In her graduate work at Queensland University of Technology, she explored the socialization of teachers into the early childhood profession.

Cynthia Colbert is chair of the Art Education Division and professor of art at the University of South Carolina in Columbia, where she holds the Louise Fry Scudder Professorship of Liberal Arts. In addition, she is an art teacher in a magnet elementary school with an interdisciplinary, inquiry-based curriculum and is completing a five-year study of the artistic development of children in her classroom.

Carmel Diezmann lectures in the School of Early Childhood at Queensland University of Technology in Brisbane, Australia. She is an experienced science educator who regularly works in schools with teachers and children. Her research interests include science and mathematics education, and the education of young gifted children.

Susan Grieshaber is a senior lecturer in the School of Early Childhood, Queensland University of Technology. Her research interests include gender and families, early childhood curriculum, and early childhood policy.

Margaret Henry began her career by publishing two thrillers. She then worked as an educational researcher with Australian Indigenous families and as a teacher of young children. More recently, she has lectured on early development and family-professional relationships in the School of Early Childhood at Queensland University of Technology.

Kym Irving is a lecturer in educational and developmental psychology in the School of Learning and Development at Queensland University of Technology. Her teaching and research interests include the development of computer-based learning materials for preservice teachers, child and adolescent social development, and children's rights.

Kerry Mallan is a senior lecturer in the School of Cultural and Language Studies at Queensland University of Technology. Her teaching and research interests are in the fields of children's literature, storytelling, discourse analysis, and gender studies. She has published widely in these areas nationally and internationally. Her most recent book is *In the Picture: Perspectives on Picture Book Art and Artists.*

Barbara Piscitelli is a senior lecturer in the School of Early Childhood at Queensland University of Technology. A longtime advocate of social change for children, Barbara's research and teaching focuses on philosophy and practice in early childhood education, particularly in the visual arts.

Anastasia P. Samaras is an associate professor and director of teacher education at Catholic University of America in Washington, D.C. Her research and practice involve a self-study of a Vygotskian interpretation in teacher preparation and interdisciplinary teaching, including the arts.

Martha Taunton is area coordinator of the art education program and an associate professor of art education at the University of Massachusetts in Amherst. Her research and writing focus on the artistic development of young children and art curriculum development. She is a coauthor with Cynthia Colbert of *Adventures in Art: Kindergarten and Developmentally Appropriate Practices for the Visual Arts Education of Young Children.*

Cassandra Weddell lectures in the School of Early Childhood at Queensland University of Technology. Her research and professional practice interests focus on aesthetics, children's festivals, live performance, and children's television.

Contents

Creating Communities for Learning

Nicola Yelland and Susan Grieshaber

INTRODUCTION

Inside Out and Outside In

This volume presents a collection of ideas that illustrate teaching practices designed to effect deeper and more meaningful understandings in the lifelong learning of early childhood professionals. At the core of the book is the notion that those who work with young children have the potential to shape the children's lives in particular ways and in a variety of contexts. Thus, the book is concerned with learning and teaching in early childhood environments.

The chapters that follow present a variety of teaching approaches that have created potent learning experiences for students and practicing professionals. All of these approaches were designed to equip participants to become more flexible in their ways of teaching and learning and to acquire an intimacy with the material that they may not previously have had. The ideas presented reflect a philosophy of early childhood education that is grounded in active learning, inquiry, and problem solving, embedded in a social and cultural context. Teachers become more reflective practitioners when they recognize how their actions and decisions in the classroom are grounded in the multiplic-

ity of life experiences they bring to it—their backgrounds, beliefs, frustrations, dreams, and desires. Teachers' work is also based on building a knowledge base within a social context that affects in complex ways what the teachers do and how they react to various situations.

One challenge of working in an early childhood setting is learning to work in relationships where ownership of the learning process is a shared experience (Cuffaro 1995). Effectiveness in a community in which individuals work together to enhance learning requires that practitioners learn about working in transactional relationships. Fostering such relationships as part of the teaching and learning process runs counter to previous learning experiences for many people, particularly those whose experiences have involved mostly transmission models of teaching. Providing opportunities for practitioners to learn about relationships of shared power and acceptance of personal responsibility for learning is an important component of both preservice and inservice programs and an integral part of learning to work with children, other staff, and families in all early childhood settings.

The chapters in this book present various ways of involving teachers in their own learning. Behind the development of these approaches is the rejection of traditional approaches, such as the transmission model (Kohlberg & Mayer 1972; Renshaw 1995), in which the teacher directs large-group lectures and tutorials that "transmit" knowledge to passive learners. These approaches are notoriously unsuccessful at preparing student teachers in many of the practical aspects needed for teaching, including even a basic skill such as managing a group of children while telling a story.

Another rationale for this volume is to enrich our understanding of what it means to be an early childhood educator (Barbour 1990). Both preservice and inservice participants require opportunities to engage in practical experiences and to learn from relationships in which shared searches for understanding are valued and supported. The chapters that follow afford an insight into how those searches have occurred in many different ways and how, through experiencing them, participants are able to enrich their own understanding of the teaching-learning relationship.

Training grounds shift and paradigm changes

Over the years, preparing professionals—not only teachers, but also doctors and lawyers—has shifted from the places where they ordinarily practice to institutions of learning, such as universities. Persistent tensions between theoretical and practical aspects of programs have resulted in calls for a new blend of theory and practice. One approach is a sort of apprenticeship in which individuals are employed in early childhood programs where they learn, by participating, how to work effectively with young children (Resnick 1987). Resnick has indeed suggested,

New forms of training for competent functioning in various kinds of work need to be developed. Ways must be found to reintroduce key elements of traditional apprenticeship in forms appropriate for modern conditions of work. (p. 17)

In this climate, understanding the ways in which people learn in environments other than formal educational institutions becomes fundamental, and from that understanding, we can change our existing programs to make the preparation and continued learning of early childhood professionals more effective. As Resnick (1987) emphasized, "School should focus its efforts on preparing people to be good *adaptive* learners, so that they can perform effectively when situations are unpredictable and task demands change" (p. 18). This adaptability is especially important in the education of teachers, who have to react on a daily basis to the individual needs, interests, and learning capabilities of a large number of children.

For many years, the predominant paradigm for describing the ways in which children learn has been the developmental theory of Jean Piaget (1951), who maintained that children's learning and reasoning were qualitatively different at various stages of their development. Piaget (1953, 1961) postulated four stages of development, invariant in sequence. In each stage, the child's behavior was determined by the application of actions available to the learner at that stage. The theory described the processes of *assimilation, accommodation,* and *equilibration,* mechanisms by which children progressed from one stage to the next. Progress was achieved through interactions with materials and other people.

Although many early childhood programs still take Piaget's constructivism as their guiding theoretical compass, more recently the social constructivist model of Vygotsky (1978) has become influential in shaping early childhood practice. The Vygotskian approach recognizes the importance of the social context of learning and the wealth of knowledge and ideas that learners bring to each new learning context. Vygotsky distinguished between the social and individual planes of thinking and learning. In the former, learners are guided by the instruction of others; in the latter, they learn of their own volition.

Initial learning takes place on a social plane, Vygotsky maintained, and through these experiences learners develop the self-regulation necessary for individual learning to occur. In this way, cognitive strategies are first encountered in an *inter*individual context during problem solving, and after they have become internalized, they become *intra*individual events. The transition from *inter* to *intra*, or from *other*-directed to *self-regulatory* behavior, was seen as mediated during the social context of learning by what has been called *scaffolding* (Wood, Bruner, & Ross 1976). Through scaffolding, learners are able to cross the *zone of proximal development*, "the distance between the actual developmental level as determined by independent problem solving and the level of potential development as determined through problem solving under adult guidance or in collaboration with more capable peers" (Vygotsky 1978, 86).

Context is central to cognition and learning

Recently, educators (e.g., Lave & Wenger 1991) have come to recognize the situation-specific (or *situated*) nature of learning and the fact that skills may not always be transferred from one context to another. Brown, Collins, and Duguid (1989) have attempted to explain why the particular activity being performed and the surrounding context are central to cognition and learning. Postulating that what constitutes appropriate, effective learning experiences varies in different situations, these researchers suggest that if we ignore the situated nature of cognition, we will defeat our goal of providing practical and robust knowledge for learners (Brown, Collins, & Duguid 1989).

According to the cognitive apprenticeship model (Brown, Collins, & Duguid 1989), learners transfer skill most readily when they have learned them through *authentic* activities—that is, the kinds of real activities in which the learners will be using the skills in the long run. For instance, to become adept at making change, learners need to go beyond paper-and-pencil problems and actually make change. Likewise, learning skills in physical and social contexts similar to those in which learners will use these skills makes transfer more likely (e.g., Lave, Murtaugh, & de la Rocha 1984). Brown, Collins, and Duguid (1989) argue that only through authentic activity and contexts do learners "gain access to the standpoint that enables practitioners to act meaningfully and purposefully. It is activity that shapes or hones their tools" (p. 36).

Cognitive apprenticeships aim to acculturate students into authentic practices by means of activities and interactions. Learning acquired in this manner is characterized by social interaction and conversation and includes solving problems collectively, displaying multiple roles, confronting ineffective strategies and misconceptions, and using collaborative work skills.

It is with such principles in mind that educators have argued that the "culture of the classroom created by outcomes based education isolates the individual from cultures which are external to the school. The extent to which this occurs successfully limits transference between the culture of the school and the community outside the school" (Grieshaber & Ashby 1997, 39). The point of interest in relation to this book is that the various contributors discuss processes that characterize the nature of learning that occurs in settings traditionally found outside the educational institution. Resnick (1987, 13–15) has argued that differences between formal classroom learning and learning in the apprenticeship context occur as a result of a variety of contrasting features:

• individual cognition in school versus shared cognition outside,

• pure mental activity in school versus the manipulation of tools outside,

• symbol manipulation in school versus contextualized reasoning outside,

• generalized learning in school versus situation-specific learning outside.

In establishing teaching and learning environments, many early childhood educators have incorporated characteristics of learning that Resnick says occur outside the formal classroom setting. Strategies by which outside-of-school learning can be successfully integrated into preservice and inservice learning experiences for early childhood educators form the basis of many chapters in this book. Examples are given of how situation-specific learning and teaching encourage shared cognition and of how the use of artifacts and contextualized reasoning offer opportunities for learners to come to fresh understandings together. Where these features appear in preservice and inservice professional development, the chances of participants transferring skills to their classroom practice is heightened. Skills that are valued by both the community and the work settings in which early childhood educators function are also more likely to be applied than those that are not valued.

Resnick (1987) has outlined what she believes are the essential elements of effective programs, namely,

• socially shared intellectual work that is organized around the joint accomplishment of tasks, so that elements of the work take on meaning in the context of the whole; and

• elements of apprenticeship that bring hidden processes to the forefront; encourage participation, observation, and commentary; and

afford the opportunity for skills to be built up gradually so that novices can participate because of the shared and social nature of the tasks involved.

Resnick contends that these elements are reflected in out-of-school cognitive performance and suggests that their structure should be organized around particular bodies of knowledge and interpretation rather than general abilities. In that way, (1) discussions of content will be tailored to engage participants in creating meaning and interpreting ideas, (2) there will be a place for critical reflection, and (3) the content of the programs will be sensitive to context-dependent nuances. According to Resnick (1987),

> If we value reason and reflection in social, political, or personal life, we must maintain a place devoted to learning how to engage in this extremely important process. School, at its best, is such a place. There reasoning and reflection can be cultivated, and a shared cultural knowledge that permits a population to function as a true society can be developed. (p. 19)

Transferable practices as catalysts for innovation

The chapters in this volume describe practices as they were used in specific contexts, yet these stories and experiences may be transferred to many other situations and serve as catalysts for innovation. Early childhood educators gain their professional skill in a multiplicity of different contexts. They may train on the job or follow an accredited course of study ranging from two to four years in an undergraduate or graduate program. Some teachers may need to study in a graduate program to become certified in their country or state. As a requirement of employment, early childhood educators may need to participate in professional development activities. These experiences not only enable early childhood educators to keep abreast of the latest research and ideas, but also ensure the profession's continued commitment to quality programs for all young children.

Listening to student voices

The book is separated into three parts. The first, "Listening to Student Voices," is concerned with giving students a voice and providing scaffolding for their learning. In this section, we are concerned with the fact that, as professionals, we create programs based on research and our personal knowledge and experience. An important part of this process is that we should be continually evaluating what we are doing to ensure a match between our actions and the ways in which students experience content and processes.

In Chapter 1, Cynthia á Beckett describes the establishment of an undergraduate student forum in a university context. She suggests that this innovation in the communication process between university staff and students facilitated the creation of a community of educators who complemented the students' understandings and learning processes in the formal part of the program. Á Beckett describes the mechanisms by which the forums created effective collaboration based on respect for the contribution of all participants in the learning exchange.

Anastasia Samaras reflects on her role as a teacher educator in Chapter 2 and describes how she has changed her practice to incorporate Vygotskian theory—in particular, the idea of providing scaffolding for learning. Her work illustrates the dynamic ways in which the learning process can be enriched and made more meaningful for students when they are given opportunities to share their cognitions with peers and teachers.

In Chapter 3, Nicola Yelland and Jenny Cartmel describe the role of the practicum in a graduate program designed to cater to the needs of qualified, experienced certified teachers seeking a specialty in early childhood education. The chapter describes not only the innovative structure of the practicum, but also how the program was run and students were supervised. Students tell stories that illustrate the ways in which the practicum assisted them in becoming early childhood professionals with a clear philosophy of learning and teaching.

Developing meaningful learning opportunities

The second part of the book, "Developing Meaningful Learning Opportunities," focuses on ways in which early childhood educators can develop meaningful learning opportunities for students in a wide variety of contexts. We reflect this focus in the title of this introduction, which is intended to convey the idea that we need to bring the *outside* (the community, or social context) *in* (to the schools) and then take the *inside* (school learning) *out* (into our communities). That is the way we share ideas.

Barbara Piscitelli discusses the principles of active learning and the ways in which they are important to the preparation and development of early childhood professionals. In Chapter 4, examples are drawn from the author's personal teaching experiences, as well as from those of other practicing professionals, and illustrate the ways in which they have explored learning experiences, playing, creative thinking, and finding and solving problems. Finally, the chapter demonstrates how adults can transfer what they have learned to a variety of early childhood contexts, such as child care centers, family child care programs, and after-school care programs.

The development of skills in literacy and numeracy is fundamental to those interested in the education of young children and the preparation of teachers and others who work with them. Carmel Diezmann and Nicola Yelland in Chapter 5 examine the process of developing the foundations of numeracy with young children. They stress the need for a broad conceptualization of numeracy and describe early mathematical experiences that can be organized for a more effective understanding of mathematical concepts and operations. The chapter examines the skills needed to function effectively in the twenty-first century and suggests ways in which early childhood educators can assist children in developing such skills in school, so that they can be applied to real-world contexts.

In Chapter 6, Kerry Mallan discusses teaching storytelling in programs for preservice and professional development and presents innovative ways of sharing stories, a fundamental activity that parents, caregivers, and teachers frequently engage in with young children. Mallan has worked with many students and teachers to increase their confidence in telling stories and to enhance their understanding and knowledge of stories from different cultures. The chapter first presents the rationale for using stories and storytelling with children and for encouraging their active participation in the construction and telling of stories of their own and of others. Mallan describes the storytelling courses that she has developed and offers practical ways that early childhood educators can use the media to enhance the lives of young children and their caregivers.

Effective early childhood practices in the visual arts are described by Martha Taunton and Cynthia Colbert in Chapter 7. Based on what early childhood educators need to know and do to create a lively art-rich program, the authors go on to describe the importance of preservice and inservice professional development for teachers.

Kym Irving's Chapter 8 outlines a project in which she developed a set of computer-based interactive multimedia materials to assist students and professionals in becoming more skilled in their observations of young children's language and social and cognitive development. Irving describes the content and documents the ways in which the materials were used in the teaching process. She sets forth the advantages of using technology to enhance one's understanding and develop one's skills in the processes of becoming an effective early childhood educator.

Creating communities for learning

In Part 3, "Creating Communities for Learning," the three chapters are concerned with ways to develop and enhance the continuing education of early childhood professionals.

In Chapter 9, Susan Grieshaber and Carmel Diezmann pose the challenge of teaching and learning science with young children and document two aspects of a large professional development program in science for educators that was implemented in a university by an early childhood professional organization. The authors describe how this inservice program enabled early childhood educators to move beyond the narrow understanding they had of science to a richer, more fruitful view. Also discussed are the implications of the program for undergraduate and on-the-job training of early childhood educators, most of whom are women.

In Chapter 10, Anna Bower examines working with parents of children who have special needs. She identifies specific issues and knowledge that have been incorporated into preservice experiences that help students become more sensitive to families' strengths and needs. Along the way, she discusses how these experiences help students learn to facilitate communication and understanding.

In the final chapter, Margaret Henry discusses strategies for working with parents and the community. The strategies arose as part of her work with preservice and inservice participants. She highlights the key role of early childhood professionals in establishing and maintaining partnerships with parents and offers examples of approaches to help students develop the skills and understandings to do so.

In this book, we consider ways to give early childhood educators opportunities to develop and update their skills for working with young children in a variety of contexts. We also encourage them to take a broader perspective, reaching outside of the school or center and into the community and beyond. The 11 chapters reflect our basic tenet that it is important to involve people in their own learning and that, to do so effectively, we must take into account characteristics of learning and teaching that occur in contexts other than school. The professionals who contributed these chapters have shared experiences that exemplify this belief.

We hope that readers who work with young children will be motivated to reflect on their own teaching practice and examine the learning opportunities and contexts that they, too, have created.

References

Barbour. N. 1990. Issues in the preparation of early childhood teachers. In *Continuing issues in early childhood education*, ed. C. Seefeldt. Columbus, OH: Merrill.

Brown, J.S., A. Collins, & P. Duguid. 1989. Situated cognition and the culture of learning. *Educational Researcher* 18 (4): 32–42.

Cuffaro, H.K. 1995. *Experimenting with the world: John Dewey and the early childhood classroom*. New York: Teachers College Press.

Grieshaber, S., & G. Ashby. 1997. Cognition, culture, and curricula: An early childhood perspective. *Journal of Cognitive Education* 6 (1): 39–52.

Kohlberg, L., & R. Mayer. 1972. Development as the aim of education. *Harvard Educational Review* 42 (4): 449–96.

Lave, J., M. Murtaugh, & O. de la Rocha. 1984. The dialectic of arithmetic in grocery shopping. In *Everyday cognition: Its development in social context*, eds. B. Rogoff & J. Lave, 67–94. Cambridge, MA: Harvard University Press.

Lave, J., & E. Wenger. 1991. *Situated cognition: Legitimate peripheral participation*. New York: Cambridge University Press.

Piaget, J. 1951. *Play, dreams, and imitation in childhood*. New York: Norton.

Piaget, J. 1953. *The origins of intellect*. London: Routledge & Kegan Paul.

Piaget, J. 1961. *The child's conception of number*. New York: Humanities.

Renshaw, P. 1995. Excellence in teaching and learning. In *External environmental scan*, 27–33. Queensland, Australia: Department of Education.

Resnick, L.B. 1987. Learning in school and out. *Educational Researcher* 16 (9): 13–20.

Vygotsky, L. 1978. *Mind in society: The development of higher psychological processes*. Cambridge, MA: Harvard University Press.

Wood, D.J., J.S. Bruner, & G. Ross. 1976. The role of tutoring in problem solving. *Journal of Child Psychology and Psychiatry* 17: 89–100.

Listening to Student Voices

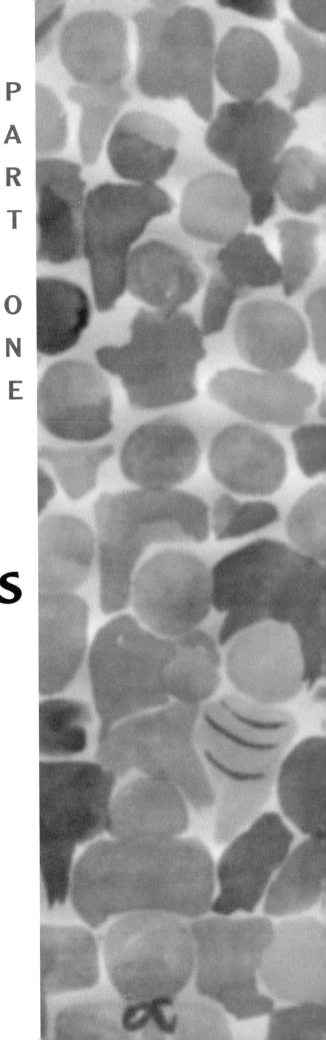

Cynthia à Beckett

Forum Groups: Creating Opportunites for Empowerment and Collaboration

Voices are raised in a shrill, excited tone. "Yes, it is, Raphael. Can't you see, it's breaking out . . . Look at it."

"No, Sophie, it can't. It's only a caterpillar."

"Yes, but Raphael, look *. . . Look now, it's really changed."*

The sound of five excited young voices and two adult voices fills the air. The speakers are in an early childhood classroom, sitting in a tight circle on child-size chairs. All are bent forward, staring, as a wanderer butterfly emerges from its silver chrysalis. The magic moment is accompanied by intense discussion between the children and the two adults, a teacher and a parent. The children lead the adults, who reflect the children's excitement. It is hard to distinguish adult from child as each participates in the rich discussion that flows freely. Through the children's reactions to this sparkling miracle of life—the metamorphosis from caterpillar to butterfly—we are transported back to our own childhood.

The story of Sophie, Raphael, and their friends in an early childhood center demonstrates the process of responsive dialogue that lies at the core of early childhood education. Children and adults were "participating in this pool of common meaning . . . in which no speaker is excluded" (Bohm 1985, 175).

The benefits of responsive dialogue extend to other contexts as well, such as the university. For example, the university setting in which I coordinated student-teacher forum groups profited from this type of dialogue. Indeed, that setting forms the basis for the early childhood education story to be told in this chapter.

The story unfolds in three parts. First, I explain what a forum is and present a sample of my experiences with student forums. Second, I discuss the issue of power as it relates to interactions taking place in the forum. Finally, I examine issues of social justice as they relate to conducting responsive dialogues in early childhood education.

Student forum groups

The term *forum* suggests an opportunity for open discussion. In its earliest use, according to the *New Shorter Oxford Dictionary*, forum refers to an assembly place, such as a market, where public discussion can take place in an open atmosphere in which debate is possible. The term *student forum* combines the notion of an open discussion with the role of students studying in a college or university. It suggests that students will have the opportunity to present their views and debate general issues that affect their educational institution.

For the purposes of this chapter, a student forum is an open meeting in which elected student representatives and educational staff hold roundtable discussions on a regular basis. Participants have the opportunity to raise and openly pursue issues they believe are important for them personally and professionally.

An early example

My own experience of student forum groups started many years ago when I was an undergraduate studying early childhood education. I was elected by my fellow students to join a committee in which students met with staff and shared ideas, raised issues of concern, and coordinated various college activities. After a number of weekly meetings, the committee decided to invite a community representative to sit in on the discussion. Before long, a range of community people had joined us, and the meetings became less routine and more engaging. The feeling of ownership and the sense that we could institute real change were compelling experiences for us students.

Many years later, as a university educator, I looked for the opportunity to enable students to participate in decisionmaking. During weekly classes, I encouraged students to speak openly and share their learning experiences. Still, I felt that this did not give them enough ownership of the process.

The opportunity to extend my interest in student participation came when a forum system was established at my institution in response to issues raised by students. I became responsible for the forum groups for students in the second year of their undergraduate early childhood teaching qualification. The forum consisted of twelve elected students representing ten tutorial groups. We arranged a time to meet outside of regular classes, and I offered to supply refreshments to facilitate a relaxed atmosphere.

During the first few sessions, we raised mainly practical issues such as increasing library resources in the early childhood education area and improving food in the canteen. I gave the students feedback after speaking with the relevant staff. The students were free to raise any issue they wanted to in our meetings, except for specific problems between a staff member and a student.

Over the months that followed, the students raised many different issues. Our tentative start was replaced by energetic, wide-ranging discussions and various recommendations. One valuable recommendation came from the third-year forum group in response to the policy of assigning a numeric grade to the professional teaching practicum, as opposed to a designation of pass or fail. The group argued that teachers in the field who were responsible for grading had many different views about the practicum, and therefore the assignment of specific grades was subjective and context bound.

After much discussion between forum groups and other students and staff, the policy was changed: teachers no longer would grade practicum teaching numerically but would rate the students' work as *satisfactory* or *unsatisfactory*. This system has remained and is considered more equitable and suitable for preservice students in early childhood education programs.

Building a student forum group

The processes described here, established some years ago, are still used and considered effective. Forum meetings stimulate thought and enable all involved to share ideas in a more collegial way than as lecturer and student.

Although each forum group operates differently, depending on its composition and agenda, all the groups have a common starting point and some basic steps that they follow during the year.

Staff involvement. Reflections and discussions about the staff's understanding of student forum groups is a strategic starting point. Sharing ideas about the value of the groups ensures a general staff commitment to the principle of giving students a voice. As new staff members join an institution, the discussions are revisited so that all involved can recommit themselves to the system. Elected staff take responsibility for coordinating the groups and provide feedback to nonparticipating students about issues raised during meetings.

Student information. At the end of large group lectures and tutorials, staff members offer information about the forum and an invitation to become a student representative. Students are invited to ask questions about the forum and think about whether they would be interested in representing their class.

Election of student forum representatives. Tutorial groups (classes or some other units in institutions not using the tutorial system) are given time to select their representatives, and the names are passed on to the staff forum coordinator.

Meeting times and guidelines. Each staff forum coordinator is responsible for arranging suitable meeting times outside students' regular class times. At the first meeting, the general procedures are established and become the group's guidelines. The time, place, and duration of meetings are determined, and the positions of minutes taker and chair are filled.

Standard conduct of meetings. Each focus group reflects a different approach, but all groups allow students to raise a range of issues and ensure that information about the discussion is communicated to other students and staff. At the next meeting, student representatives and staff discuss any responses they have received, thus supporting the communication process.

End-of-year closure. At the end of each teaching year, the staff thank the students and give them each a letter detailing their contributions. The groups disband, and new ones are formed the following year. Some students then may choose to become involved again.

Follow-up. The activities of forum groups extend collegiate links between student groups and between students and staff. These links may lead to additional student activities outside the scope of the forum group mandate. For example, one group in my institution established an early childhood club.

Two years after the forum groups began, students started talking about how to extend the forum activities and become more independent. They decided to form a professional early childhood club for interested students and staff. Through this club they would organize workshops, speakers, and events to enhance their professional life as new teachers. This successful organization has continued to evolve and grow.

Creating a community

Being involved in student forum groups is both exciting and complex. Through the responsive dialogue, participants create their own community. Students raise issues openly, follow their current interests, and discuss matters of general concern. At their best, student forum groups in a college or university share elements of the early childhood classroom scene described at the start of this chapter. The students' excitement will be obvious as issues are bandied about, discussion flows freely, and the contributions of the participants are appreciated.

My experience with student forum groups over the years has enabled me to be part of a community. Moore (1996) argues that we can find community only "where we have the opportunity to be full individuals . . . [where community is about] a life quickened with the pleasure of living with a common will and purpose." Community is also about "taking pleasure in others' success and well-being" (213–14). In today's postindustrial world, it is difficult to have a sense of connection and to feel that others either listen or care. In the student forums, by contrast, the responsive dialogue ensures listening and caring.

My student forum experiences were so positive and constructive that I sought to extend them to other contexts.

Tailoring the format to other education contexts. My area of specialization is contemporary family issues and early childhood education. When I was asked to design a new course on this subject, I sought student participation.

I invited students to elect two representatives to join other faculty members and myself in designing the new course. We worked together for some months, and the meetings were so productive that we asked the student representatives if they would continue to meet with us when the course began. The students consented and joined faculty at weekly organizational meetings. They contributed to the discussions, raised issues about the course with the students who were taking it, and gave feedback to staff and students. This type of university teaching was stimulating and satisfying, and it enhanced the quality of the course in many ways.

Modeling early childhood education values. A university setting can be remote and impersonal. In fact, it often seems to be in direct contrast to the principles of early childhood education taught in our method and curriculum courses. Forum groups seem to counterbalance this remoteness and actually model the aspects of early childhood education we advocate.

Forum groups appeal to both staff and students, and support for the concept seems widespread. In part, this support appears to come from a commitment to principles of equity that underlie effective early childhood programs in which all children and adults are valued and each child is accorded equal access to learning opportunities.

The effective early childhood education program seeks to tailor learning experiences and social interactions to the needs of each child, family, and teacher. This form of interaction does not take place under a rigid set of rules and regulations; rather, it is undertaken in a spirit of acting together, enhanced by strategies and guidelines set in place by caring staff. The opportunity for students to participate in such a dialogue is made possible by the willingness of those in a position of power to listen to others.

Issues of power

In exploring student forum groups, issues of power—who is heard and who is allowed to speak—come into focus. Some would argue that inviting students to be part of a student forum or, in an early childhood setting, encouraging parents to share in program planning (à Beckett 1990) is about those with power appearing to listen to those without power, but not taking any real notice.

It could also be argued that the apparent democratic process in the forum groups is an idealistic fabrication, because each situation is individually negotiated, and individuals are positioned variously in terms of their abilities to participate in this negotiation process.

In a university setting, furthermore, students are instructed through *rituals of exclusion* (Foucault 1989). Foucault argues that through rituals of exclusion, such as examinations, universities socially construct individuals and thus alienate them from their original communities.

While these arguments must be acknowledged, so must our desire for change that promotes equitable outcomes. Many faculty and students have found that the forum groups tend to promote more equitable dialogues and situations in which people demonstrate a genuine regard for one another.

Facilitating change in faculty-student relations

Student forum groups in the university should aim to change the power relation between student and teacher. Game and Metcalfe (1996) emphasize the benefits that result from creating a new climate in which students are more autonomous. The newfound freedom enables participants to cooperate more easily with one another and staff.

Harris (1999) has also explored these issues through a program that offers a bachelor's degree in early childhood education. The program allows students more freedom in selecting their courses of study, and the students, in turn, report that they feel a real sense of ownership of the curriculum and of their own learning.

Engendering mutual trust and respect. In the early childhood education setting, teachers and university professors can do much to alter power relations and create good communication systems. However, they must be aware that it is not enough just to create opportunities for communicative dialogue; those in power also must win the others' trust.

Social theorist Habermas (1987) has argued that sharing of power is possible if there is a genuine exchange between individuals despite the technical rationalism that many believe dominates and dehumanizes public arenas. Habermas is concerned about a truthful exchange of ideas according to the principles of "communicative competence."

Preston and Symes (1992) explore Habermas's ideas and argue for educational settings that create a community of learners linked by a genuine regard for each other. Preston and Symes emphasize that educators who strive for democratic learning environments can make a positive difference through transformative, emancipatory models of education.

Giving students a voice. Student forum groups in universities and colleges are fundamentally about altering the dominant structures so that institutions become less hierarchical. Forum groups are concerned with ensuring that each person has a voice and it is appreciated. Forums let students understand that they are being heard and that their contribution is appreciated. The alienation associated with universities is deconstructed in a student forum group.

Democratic characteristics of forums

Of course, the process of establishing meaningful forum groups and the actual form the groups take will vary from institution to institution and from country to country, but all forums have some core features, including

• a demonstrable equitable practice based on respect for others,

• mutual appreciation and understanding among the participants,

• demonstrations of trust, and

• opportunities for collaboration.

Duff, Brown, and Van Scoy (1995) identify trust and mutual respect as key elements in assisting early childhood staff to be effective in their work in the field. Presenting forum groups to early childhood education students will aid them in their professional preparation. When the core features of respect, understanding, trust, and collaboration are present, an atmosphere is created in which democratic practice and social justice can flourish.

The elements of respect, equity, and social justice are neither as linear nor as rigid as they may appear to be. They assist us in making sense of ourselves and one another when working together in early childhood education. Collaboration, mutual appreciation, and trust can be viewed as sentimental or even empty, unless we identify their roles in our daily lives. Once we do, they can help us create respectful and equitable learning settings.

Wider issues of social justice

The topic of social justice and human rights may seem far removed from the issue of student voices in a university context. However, in early childhood education, we are bound professionally and ethically to investigate such topics.

Early childhood education has a traditional involvement with equitable practice and social justice. In Australia, for example, many early childhood centers were established at the turn of the century to care for destitute children from families badly hit by the depression of the 1890s. Sebastian-Nickell and Milne (1992) explain the relation in these terms:

> Social justice has permeated many activities and methods in early education programs for over 100 years. The early childhood tradition—the valuing of individual differences and of early social development—reflects the centrality of notions of social justice. (p. 115)

This climate can also exist in colleges or universities preparing adults for work in early childhood education settings.

Sebastian-Nickell and Milne (1992) also provide a comprehensive definition of social justice that is applicable to early childhood education:

> Social justice involves the principle that all persons are of equal value and that they have the right to equality of treatment and opportunity whatever their differences of race, culture, gender, religion, physical prowess, intellectual talent. (p. 115)

Social justice in an early childhood education setting can be further understood by expanding the notion beyond small local communities. For instance, every nation will have some variation in the way it defines the key issues associated with equity and social justice. Australia is a case in point. The Australian government (Sebastian-Nickell & Milne 1992, 115) states that a socially just Australia is one in which there is

• a fair distribution of economic resources;

• equal access to essential services such as housing, health care, and education;

• equal rights in civil, legal, and industrial affairs; and,

• equal opportunity for participation by all in personal development and community life and decisionmaking.

The last of these points refers to real participation in personal development, community life, and decisionmaking, and it is particularly relevant to the goal of equity that is aimed at in most

early childhood education settings through a trusting relationship that promotes collaboration.

Toward the future

Whatever aspect of early childhood education we are involved in, we have the opportunity to create a responsive community—a place in which individuals, such as Raphael and Sophie, can really experience the magic of the emerging butterfly. As early childhood educators, we can build bridges, forge bonds, and create a forum for sharing our experiences. Through student forum groups, we can address issues of power in a university setting to create genuine opportunities for democratic learning. Finally, as early childhood educators, we can create environments that engender trust, respect, and collaboration—environments that offer students opportunities to give voice to their reflections, feelings, and aspirations.

References

à Beckett, C. 1990. Parent/staff relationships. In *Trusting toddlers*, ed. A. Stonehouse, 128–41. St. Paul, MN: Toys 'n' Things.

Bohm, D. 1985. *Unfolding meaning*. London: Routledge.

Duff, E., M. Brown, & J. Van Scoy. 1995. Reflection and self-evaluation: Keys to professional development. *Young Children* 50 (4): 81–88.

Foucault, M. 1989. *Foucault live*. New York: Semiotext(e).

Game, A., & A. Metcalfe. 1996. *Passionate sociology*. London: Sage.

Habermas, J. 1987. *The theory of communicative action, volume 2: The critique of functionalist reason.* Cambridge, UK: Polity.

Harris, P. 1999. "We own what we're doing": Developing preservice early childhood teachers as researchers. *Journal of Australian Research in Early Childhood Education* (1): 72–84.

Moore, T. 1996. *The education of the heart*. Rydalmere, Australia: Hodder & Stroughton.

Preston, N., & C. Symes. 1992. *Schools and classrooms: A cultural analysis of education*. Melbourne, Australia: Longman Cheshire.

Sebastian-Nickell, P. & R. Milne. 1992. *Care and education of young children*. Melbourne, Australia: Longman Cheshire.

Anastasia P. Samaras

Scaffolding Preservice Teachers' Learning

It was the end of another semester of student teaching. Student teachers gathered in the now familiar circle of discussion to share what they had learned from their course work and field experiences. An early childhood education student comments freely that her cooperating teacher told her to forget everything she learned in education methods courses and that practice was the most useful ingredient in learning to teach.

Unfortunately, a review of the literature on learning to teach reaffirms that this viewpoint is not atypical (Feiman-Nemser & Buchmann 1985; Lanier & Little 1986; Sarason, Davidson, & Blatt 1986; Britzman & Greene 1991). Accordingly, we can ask, What's missing in teacher preparation? How can educators help preservice teachers become effective teachers of young children? How can educators improve their own teaching practices?

An essential component of innovation in curricula for teacher preparation arises by considering teaching as a "heart-felt, mind-informed, research-driven commitment" that typically runs counter to the mission of research institutions (Knowles & Cole 1998, 22).

As a self-study teacher educator, one who critically examines actions and their context for the purpose of instilling a more consciously driven mode of professional activity in teachers, I research and write about my teaching practice (Samaras, Taylor, & Kelly 1994; Samaras 1995a, 1998, in press; Samaras & Gismondi 1998; Samaras & Wilson 1999). Much of my work involves research on the subject of interdisciplinary teaching teams, from the perspective of a sociocultural or Vygotskian approach to preparing early childhood and elementary education preservice teachers (Vygotsky 1978, 1981).

Although I have adapted some of Vygotsky's work to my own, I am becoming my own theoretician, with artistic experiences always in a state of becoming (Langer 1953). By way of illustration, I worked with a dance and physical education specialist and a kindergarten teacher and her class to teach preservice teachers how to incorporate movement into a curriculum (Samaras, Straits, & Patrick 1998). I teamed with a drama professor in an interdisciplinary course, Drama beyond the Theatre, to teach preservice teachers how to apply drama in their classrooms (Samaras with Reed 2000).

To further support preservice teachers' professional development, in this chapter I revisit my logs and writings to reconstruct my experiences as a seasoned teacher educator and to note my inquiry into teaching practices as an innovator. The following three sections of the chapter focus on (1) the need for innovation by teacher educators in the context of contemporary educational reform, (2) the implications of Vygotskian tenets for teaching and research, and (3) a restructured early childhood and elementary teacher education program that embodies a Vygotskian approach. After these discussions are preservice teachers' reflections about their experiences in such a program. In conclusion, I consider the ways in which this approach has improved practice and has implications for other early childhood professionals.

Reform and innovation

Calls for large-scale, comprehensive educational reform and standards for students and teachers are becoming a part of the political and social landscape. Of course, reform movements are not a novel enterprise and continue to be riddled with problems, including the capability to distract us from an evolving education culture that affords professional opportunities for lifelong learning (Eisner 1998). But the current reform movement that critiques the quality of teacher education programs challenges teacher educators to think about their professional role (see Knowles & Cole 1998, for a review of teacher education reform). Issues of accountability, accreditation, and assessment continue to affect the teaching profession and call into question how teachers of young children are prepared. Teacher educators cannot ignore the outside world as they teach from inside their ivory towers.

The current pressures of systemic reform and performance-based accountability, coupled with the reality of teacher shortages and attrition, present new dilemmas for the profession. Nationally, nearly half of new teachers leave the profession within their first five years (Darling-Hammond 1997). Now, more than ever, innovative teaching practices are needed in preparing teachers to be lifelong learners practicing their passion. Reform, or "mak[ing] things better by removing faults and defects" (*Webster's New World Dictionary of American Language*, 2d college edition), is neither limited to, nor necessarily influenced by, top-down legislative mandates; small-scale innovations and grassroots efforts by educators may actually expedite reform, because they can empower those who seek to change things.

This chapter is about one such grassroots effort—an innovation that places what is talked about in Vygotskian theory in the context of preservice teachers' learning.

Tracing my steps

My professional work embodying a sociocultural approach to teaching began when I was a graduate research assistant participating in one of the first national studies investigating the impact of computers on young children. I logged observations of pairs of young children working with different teachers on a computer, seeking to unveil the cognitive and affective potentials of computer usage (Wright & Samaras 1986).

On further investigation, I began to delineate the teacher's role in unleashing children's potential. The timed logs indicated that the children stayed longer at the computer and were creative when the teacher gave suggestions and prompts rather than directives. I would later discover that the teacher's facilitation and scaffolded instruction—tailoring instruction to what children could achieve, with gradations of support and with general and specific statements—was related to the children's problem-solving techniques, use of strategy, and self-regulation (Samaras 1991, 1995b). Teaching 3-year-olds at a university laboratory preschool and, later, conducting on-site training with teachers in Head Start programs gave me firsthand experience in scaffolding young children's learning.

When I became a teacher educator, I decided that if I was going to teach teachers how to create supports for children's learning, I should practice what I preached. Although Vygotskian theory had been discussed in relation to young children's learning (Berk & Winsler 1995), little research investigated its application to preservice teachers' learning. Consequently, I began to sort out what seems so obvious now but was not at the time: a Vygotskian approach for teaching preservice teachers. Berlak and Berlak (1987) state, "Only as we come to view our own actions and preferences, as products of historical as well as biographical forces, rather than as natural and inevitable, can we escape the ideological assumptions that underlie teaching practices, and engage in reflective teaching" (p. 175). With the outstanding professional support I would receive from editors and colleagues, I began to examine my life as an educator and found that telling my own story helped me understand my teaching and how I applied theory (Samaras 1995a, 1998).

Vygotsky in teacher education

My teaching is based on a sociocultural theoretical model of how people learn. In much the same way as people learn in natural settings— families, communities, and the workplace (see Lave & Wenger 1991)—the premise of my teaching is that learning takes place through joint productive activity. Preservice teachers need opportunities to discuss their course learning and personal theories when problems arise *while* they are teaching and reflecting in an actual classroom. Some things simply cannot be learned out of a textbook; they need to be real and presently happening to make any sense. In Vygotskian

terms, situated cognition of course work occurs during the situated activity of fieldwork.

Socially shared cognition

Vygotsky believed that cognition is always socially mediated or influenced by others through social interaction. Higher mental functions, such as memory, attention, and self-regulation, occur in the context of a shared task definition between individuals and arise through collaboration. According to Vygotsky, thinking begins on the interpersonal, or social, plane before it is internalized as intrapersonal knowledge.

Meaning is constructed through social mediation, negotiation, and dialogue (Newman, Griffin, & Cole 1989). Socially shared cognitive formats and various forms of interaction with an audience (e.g., dyads, small groups, cohorts, and seminars) help promote preservice teachers' cognitive, affective, and collegial support (Samaras & Gismondi 1998).

Mediated learning through joint activity

Vygotskian theory states that learning occurs during actual problem-solving joint activity or shared task definition with others (Vygotsky 1981). Accordingly, preservice teachers should be given the opportunity to interact collaboratively and to assist others with skills they acquire in the context of performing a specific activity. Learning how to plan, implement, and evaluate an integrated unit with a peer and a cooperating teacher can be a shared task that necessitates the interaction. Learning can be enhanced through support systems that employ (a) problem-based learning; (b) shared responsibility; (c) gradations of free rein for experimentation; (d) structured, content-specific, contingent feedback; and (e) reflective assessments, or the bringing of attention to the ongoing action during instruction (Samaras 1991).

A work context for restructuring programs

In a deliberative, reflective teacher education program (see Valli 1990) such as I direct, undergraduate and graduate students are coached in a perspective-taking orientation toward teaching, grounded in field experience. Through inquiries regarding dilemmas they identify in practice, preservice teachers discuss actions and strategies on the basis of professional knowledge and reflection, not out of habit, tradition, or impulse.

One year, program evaluations revealed that preservice teachers perceived the field experience as unconnected to their methods courses. They had difficulty transferring skills learned in their course work to the real world of daily teaching. The field experience did not promote critical and reflective thinking about individualized learning and teaching, gave no opportunities for making decisions about the curriculum, did not apply content knowledge, and failed to incorporate long-term planning. Preservice teachers worked independently of peers in a one-day-a-week, yearlong practicum in which they completed individual course assignments for a hypothetical unit of instruction.

Upon learning of the evaluations, faculty in the program (Samaras, Taylor, & Kelly 1994; Taylor, Samaras, & Gay 1994) worked to restructure it with an eye toward the following goals:

• to provide preservice teachers with a coherent experience that allows them to see the curriculum in action—the way learning experiences build upon learning experiences,

• to give preservice teachers an opportunity to design and carry out a sequence of instruction, and

• to give preservice teachers an opportunity to learn instructional techniques from cooperating teachers and to try out practices learned in their course work.

In the restructured program, cohorts of preservice teachers complete two unique field experiences that afford increased time teaching and that include formative assessments during the second semester before student teaching. Both semesters involve field experiences concurrent with course work in methodology and with practicum seminars.

During the first semester, the students take courses in children's literature, classroom management, and curriculum and instruction that are carefully tied to a two-half-days-a-week practicum at one of two schools. The second semester involves methods courses in reading, mathematics, health and physical education, and social studies and science and includes participating in a three-half-days-a-week practicum. Together, the two semesters allow all students to teach in two different schools and also to observe and participate in the opening and closing of a school year.

A Vygotskian approach

I teach a curriculum and instruction course in the fall and a methods course in social studies and science in the spring and have taught the practicum each semester. The arrangement of teaching the same preservice teachers for one year is consistent with the Vygotskian emphasis on history and interaction to enhance knowing and scaffolding of learners, as in the Reggio Emilia system (Berk & Winsler 1995, 145). My positions as director of teacher education and coordinator of academic advising have enabled me to meet many of the preservice teachers before I teach them.

Reflecting and sharing

Influenced by the work of Bullough (1994) and Cole and Knowles (1995), I ask my students to write about their education in the first semester. After giving some highlights of my own education, I have the students present their stories in small groups in class and also share them with their cooperative teachers. In this manner, and by coding their learning preferences and teaching temperaments with the Myers–Briggs Type Indicator (Briggs & Briggs-Myers 1991), I come to know my students.

I also read and respond to students' weekly electronic logs containing their reflections on educational dilemmas they encounter in their field experiences. Using Posner's (1996) framework that encourages preservice teachers to take the perspective of others, the students record their reflections, copies of which are then sent weekly to the university field liaison and me and, intermittently, to professors of other methods courses.

In the practicum seminars, preservice teachers are expected to communicate their thoughts as they react to specific problematic situations. Their shared reflections also help prepare them for a research project they must complete during their student teaching.

Dialogues in roundtable, jigsaw, and poster session formats are a norm in my teaching. I use instructional formats of socially shared cognition (see Samaras 1998) to build professional relationships among peers through two-person and group projects and to encourage my students to challenge their own thinking. The approach relies heavily on cooperation rather than competition and helps develop an understanding of one's approach to teaching. Through their socially shared reflections, the preservice teachers develop notions of teaching and relationships with the students they work with in the schools.

Implementing and evaluating fieldwork

In the second semester, preservice teachers work in pairs to plan, implement, and evaluate an integrated unit in their practicum classroom with the guidance of a cooperative teacher. Although the integrated unit is housed within the social studies and science methods course and centers around a social studies or science theme (e.g., rain forests, communities, weather), professors from the

reading, mathematics, and health and physical education methods courses contribute to both the unit and the field experience.

The integrated unit requires preservice teachers to revisit their earlier educational experience in their course of study. For example, they demonstrate knowledge from their course work in the psychology of education in the preplanning section of the unit by discussing the theoretical assumptions they made in designing the unit. Through pre- and postconcept mapping, they evaluate how closely they came to fulfilling their plans. They also discuss human development issues in their unit (e.g., the rationale for their ideas, the appropriateness of their lessons to the developmental stages of the children they teach, and various motivational issues).

The integrated unit also requires preservice teachers to apply the prior knowledge they gained in the first semester to the second semester; for example, they describe the ethos and setting of the school in which they teach, discuss classroom management strategies, select children's literature, and use current technology. Throughout the yearlong course and fieldwork, they have the opportunity to be coached by peers and cooperating teachers and to view videotaped recordings of microteaching. Preservice teachers also shadow experts in the schools in which they teach and write about and share their observations in courses.

Extensive and ongoing data collection has resulted in numerous records of preservice teachers' field progress reports; self-, peer, and cooperative teacher assessments; narratives of their professional growth; metacognitive traces of unit planning; concept maps; audiotaped interviews; and exit conferences.

I also assess my own teaching to see what my students are learning, and preservice teachers' narratives have helped me evaluate the effectiveness of my restructured program and a Vygotskian approach to teacher preparation. One of my logs is indicative of the value of self-assessment:

I, too, reflect on course goals with the insights I have gained through my students' comments. I appreciate their willingness to reveal their thinking. When I sat down to review the stacks of data I had collected, I heard their voices and not just my own.

Students' voices and lessons learned

This section presents some of my students' comments about teaching.

Coursework and the practicum

In both their comments and exit interviews, the students repeatedly focused on the application of their course work to the practicum and how they adapted it to fieldwork. They did not, however, view their teaching as a recipe:

> We [a pair of students working together] were taking things you were teaching us in class and showing us. We altered them, applied them basically to the environment we were put in, and didn't take it just from the book. We've learned that we had to take the situation we were placed in and alter what we would get in class to that situation. And it worked.

The practicum gave them a realistic approach to teaching and to how curriculum is developed and allowed them entry, on a small scale, into a professional community:

> The classroom dynamics required us to think in depth about how we could structure our lesson plans in the unit. The environment of the class provided us with a lot of chances for trying out classroom management techniques.

Analyzing their school's ethos was a skill learned in the context of their practicum during the first semester; cohorts presented their reports in symposia. One preservice teacher expressed her disappointment with the school ethos, which she identified in her second-semester practicum placement:

> I think the school you go to, *really* determines the way students are going to end up. These kids are just having all their creativity sucked

out of them. . . . I'm beginning to be very aware of the effects of teaching that way.

Learning and teaching together

The assignments they were given required each pair of students to generate ideas, cooperate, and negotiate with each other and their cooperative teacher.

A student wrote,

> I would have liked to do a unit by myself. Just because we're different. . . . We were a big complement for each other because she relaxed me, and I got her on the ball a little bit. You definitely had different perspectives, which was good. . . . It's funny how we would interpret something that happened in the classroom. "Can you believe she did that?" [I said]. Sara [assented] but . . . would have seen it in an entirely different way.

Another said,

> From the beginning, [the cooperative teacher] forced us to figure out how we were going to organize [the integrated unit]. She sat down with us. She did the very beginning of the planning. From there we were kind of on our own, but she helped in that, the long-range planning. . . . She wanted to know exactly what we were going to cover, when we were going to cover it, and how long it would take. She gives you so much freedom, so much time.

This collegial support extended beyond the pair of students and the cooperative teacher:

> Our class was terrific. We helped each other. We were just working together, and that is something that we learned; how to teach the kids to work together. Well, that's in essence what you all were doing. . . . If it helps me, I know that it's going to help my students.

The integrated unit as a shared, authentic task

Preservice teachers indicated that the integrated unit assignment helped them bring together what they learned in course work, see the impact of their teaching, make decisions regarding the curriculum, and adjust for individual differences in their students' acquisition of knowledge. From two of the preservice teachers came

> I think actually doing the unit, doing the time, having to combine the strategies, the timing, the disciplines—all that [was valuable]. Before, everything was so separate. I would try to combine the disciplines, but it was all on paper. Then putting it all together—I wouldn't have had to do that without the unit and without the fieldwork. Almost unknowingly, I took everything from the classroom that I had learned from the book and then actually did it. . . . So later I realized, "Oh, this is what they were talking about when we learned these different strategies."

and

> What was understandable to the two of us in teaching the unit was confusing, frustrating, and difficult for our students. We came up with a method of simplifying the activity and went through it with them again, this time as a class, so that if any questions arose, we would be sure to pick up on any students who were having problems.

Conclusion

The approach presented in this chapter is not the only one to scaffolding preservice teachers' learning; rather, it is one kind of strategy applied in a specific context.

Using Vygotskian notions of learning, the restructured teacher program described herein gives preservice teachers opportunities for socially shared cognition, mediated learning, and joint activity and can lead to improved practice. Preservice teachers are able to connect their methods course work to their field experiences and, specifically, to their own students' understanding of what they are teaching. Students gain insight into how they are developing as teachers from their intellectual and affective interactions with their peers, cooperative teachers, and professors. The integrated

unit serves as the hub, or motivation, for the exchange of ideas and new understandings.

Regardless of which theory one espouses, three things are clear. First, teachers need to have a conceptual and theoretical base for their teaching (Samaras 1994). Second, preservice teachers' course work is more meaningful when it is aligned with and geared toward their fieldwork. Through such an alignment, future teachers can recognize when change is necessary and what that change should be. Third, like young children, teachers can develop a deeper understanding of what they are learning when they are given opportunities to work together sharing tasks and goals.

Present-day education is characterized by standards-driven curriculum and legislative mandates for schools and universities. Accordingly, we need to hold fast to innovations that can help us to meet those standards in effective ways. Preservice teachers are artists who must use their imaginations to find solutions through their own innovations.

Sharing ideas, mistakes, and successes with peers will bind preservice teachers together as early childhood professionals and allow them to see themselves as human beings seeking to educate those entrusted to them. They will see that they are morally responsible for making their classrooms conducive to learning. Their reforms and innovations will spur them on to becoming lifelong learners, who will not tire of the demands placed on them for continuous growth. Through their experiences, they will see that change is more likely and liberating if they have ownership in it. They may not always be successful in their efforts, but when they are, they will accentuate the value of innovation for early childhood professionals.

References

Berk, L.E., & A. Winsler. 1995. *Scaffolding children's learning: Vygotsky and early childhood education.* Washington, DC: NAEYC.

Berlak, A., & H. Berlak. 1987. Teachers working with teachers to transform schools. In *Educating teachers:*

Changing the nature of pedagogical knowledge, ed. J. Smyth. Philadelphia: Falmer.

Briggs, K.C., & I. Briggs-Myers. 1991. *Myers-Briggs type indicator.* Palo Alto, CA: Consulting Psychologists Press.

Britzman, D.P., & M. Greene. 1991. *Practice makes practice: A critical study of learning to teach.* Albany: State University of New York Press.

Bullough, R.V. 1994. When more or less is not enough: Rethinking preservice teacher education. Paper presented at the annual meeting of the American Educational Research Association, 4–8 April, New Orleans, Louisiana.

Cole, A.L., & J.G. Knowles. 1995. Methods and issues in a life history approach to self-study. In *Teachers who teach teachers: Reflections on teacher education,* eds. T. Russell & F. Korthagen, 130–51. Philadelphia: Falmer.

Darling-Hammond, L. 1997. *The right to learn: A blueprint for creating schools that work.* San Francisco: Jossey-Bass.

Eisner, E.W. 1998. *The kinds of schools we need: Personal essays.* Portsmouth, NH: Heinemann.

Feiman-Nemser, S., & M. Buchmann. 1985. Pitfalls of experience in teacher preparation. *Teachers College Record* 87 (1): 53–65.

Knowles, J.G., & A.L. Cole. 1998. Setting and defining the context of reform. In *The heart of the matter: Teacher educators and teacher education reform,* eds. A.L. Cole, R. Elijah, & J.G. Knowles, 15–36. San Francisco: Caddo Gap.

Langer, S. 1953. *Feeling and form.* New York: Scribner.

Lanier, J., & J. Little. 1986. Research on teacher education. In *Handbook of research on teaching,* 3d ed., ed. M. Wittrock, 527–69. New York: Macmillan.

Lave, J., & E. Wenger. 1991. *Situated learning: Legitimate peripheral participation.* Cambridge, UK: Cambridge University Press.

Newman, D., P. Griffin, & M. Cole. 1989. *The construction zone: Working for cognitive change in school.* Cambridge, UK: Cambridge University Press.

Posner, G.J. 1996. *Field experience: A guide to reflective teaching.* White Plains, NY: Longman.

Samaras, A.P. 1991. Transitions to competence: An investigation of adult mediation in preschoolers' self-regulation with a microcomputer-based problem-solving task. *Early Education and Development* 2 (3): 181–96.

Samaras, A.P. 1994. Show and tell those theories! *Day Care and Early Education* 2 (1): 21–23.

Samaras, A.P. 1995a. My journey to Ithaca: Reflections of a teacher educator. *Teaching Education* 7 (1): 96–101.

Samaras, A.P. 1995b. Children's computers. *Childhood Education* 72 (3): 133–36.

Samaras, A.P. 1998. Finding my way: Teaching methods courses from a sociocultural perspective. In *The heart of the matter: Teacher educators and teacher education reform,* eds. A.L. Cole, R. Elijah, & J.G. Knowles, 55–79. San Francisco: Caddo Gap.

Samaras, A.P. In press. When is a practicum productive? A study in learning to plan. *Action in Teacher Education.*

Samaras, A.P., & S. Gismondi. 1998. Scaffolds in the field: Vygotskian interpretation in a teacher education program. *Teaching and Teacher Education* 14 (7): 1–19.

Samaras, A.P. with contributions by R.L. Reed. 2000. Transcending traditional boundaries through drama: Interdisciplinary teaching and perspective-taking. Paper presented at the Annual Conference of the Self-Study in Teacher Education Practices SIG, Herstmonceux III, East Sussex, England.

Samaras, A.P., S.A. Straits, & S.S. Patrick. 1998. Collaborating through movement across disciplines and schools. *Teaching Education* 9 (2): 11–20.

Samaras, A.P., N.E. Taylor, & B. Kelly. 1994. Teachers teaching teachers. *Momentum* 25 (3): 67–71.

Samaras, A.P., & J.C. Wilson. 1999. Am I invited? Perspectives of family involvement with technology in inner-city schools. *Urban Education* 34 (4): 499–530.

Sarason, S.B., K.S. Davidson, & B. Blatt. 1986. *The preparation of teachers: An unstudied problem in education.* Cambridge, MA: Brookline.

Taylor, N.E., A.P. Samaras, & A. Gay. 1994. *Making connections: Aligning theory and field practice.* Report No. SP 035 008. Washington, DC: The Catholic University of America, Department of Education. ERIC, ED 367 597.

Valli, L. 1990. Moral approaches to reflective practice. In *Encouraging reflective practice in education,* eds. R.T. Clift, W.R. Houston, & M.C. Pugach, 39–56. New York: Teachers College Press.

Vygotsky, L.S. 1978. *Mind in society: The development of higher psychological processes.* Edited and translated by M. Cole, V. John-Steiner, S. Scribner, & E. Souberman. Cambridge, MA: Harvard University Press.

Vygotsky, L.S. 1981. The genesis of higher mental functions. In *The concept of activity in Soviet psychology,* ed. J.V. Wertsch. New York: M.E. Sharpe.

Wright, J., & A. Samaras. 1986. Play worlds and microworlds. In *Young children and microcomputers,* eds. P.F. Campbell & G.G. Fein, 73–86. Englewood Cliffs, NJ: Prentice Hall.

Nicola J. Yelland and Jenny Cartmel

3

Rethinking Professional Practice: Narratives of the Practicum

Looking at life as narrative or stories allows us to see the unities, continuities and discontinuities, images and rhythms in our lives.
—D.J. Clandinin

*I*f early childhood teacher education is to have a relevant and effective practicum component, its practitioners must be open to change, recognize the current requirements of the teaching profession, and respond to current research issues. This has been recognized in the literature (e.g., Jones 1993; Darling-Hammond 1994) and with innovative practices such as those of the Professional Development Schools Project (The Holmes Group 1990), which sparked the creation of close partnerships between public schools and universities, bringing university faculty into the schools to mentor and train teachers in the school context.

An effective practicum experience empowers students to be active, responsible learners and develop positive professional attitudes. The most significant rewards for teachers often stem from the work itself, teachers' relationships with children and other teachers, an activity done well, freedom to manage their own classrooms, and the feeling of being capable, hardworking professionals (Schools Council, NBEET, cited in Taylor 1991).

Professional development schools provide one very promising avenue for achieving such goals. In this chapter we explore additional methods demonstrated in a program at our university in which participants are already working in education or care contexts with children of various ages.

The students participating in the program are located in distant and diverse locations, which means we have to be imaginative in creating a community of learners and providing ongoing mentoring and support. New avenues for communication and students' sharing of stories from their experiences have proved to be foundation stones of the community. Students involved in the practicum have commented on the ways in which the field experience, coupled with composing and sharing narratives about the experience, has helped them to conceptualize what it means to be a teacher of young children and to engage in dialogues with teachers and others in the community.

About the program

The Graduate Diploma in Education (Early Childhood) was designed to address the needs of qualified, experienced, certified teachers seeking a specialist early childhood teaching qualification. Although they are already teachers, these degree candidates are required to complete two periods of field experience with young children. Many of the students are employed as teachers in schools, kindergartens, and childcare settings and cannot be released from their duties for the two-week period required for all practicum options. Therefore, designing and scheduling practicum experiences is a challenging task.

In the graduate program, the aim is for students to gain the knowledge required to

• understand the latest research in human development and learning in the early years;

• plan and evaluate appropriate curricula and strategies for working with young children;

• competently examine and contemplate significant issues related to the education of young children;

• formulate a philosophy of early childhood education;

• gain and demonstrate skill in interpersonal relations as they work with young children and their families, community members, colleagues, and nonteaching professionals.

The program consists of eight core subjects: development and learning from birth to 8 years, early childhood curriculum (two units), contexts of early childhood education, early childhood program planning, research in early childhood, transactions in early childhood, and the practicum experiences.

When the program was initiated, it was a specialist qualification for those who wanted to teach children in the age range of 3 to 8 years. It catered primarily to teachers who were already employed. In the first years of its operation, the main form in which the program was offered was that of twice-yearly practica during school vacations, taking place in different regions of the country. To provide options for teacher educators to consider in designing fieldwork, we describe three ways a practicum can be structured and supplemented with the use of narratives to present students' perception of the options.

A look at the practicum

As the degree program evolved and the number of participants increased, it became apparent that the practicum arrangements needed to be more flexible. To answer this need, the structure of the program was changed.

Offering choice

Three practicum options were developed to meet the varying needs and circumstances of the students:

• **Option A: School holiday program.** This practicum option is for students who are unable to meet the commitment of attending classes during the regular university semester, but who want an opportunity to teach with others in a collaborative environment. Currently, this option offers fieldwork with two different age groups: birth to 3 years and 3 to 8 years. Teams of six to eight students plan, implement, and evaluate a program with the support of an experienced early childhood educator.

• **Option B: Individual practicum.** Here, students fulfill their practicum requirements in the early childhood center of their choice, with the practicum accommodating students' individual needs and constraints, such as family and work obligations. The person supervising the practicum must be qualified in early childhood education, and a university supervisor is appointed to visit during the two-week period.

• **Option C: Special circumstances practicum.** This option affords second-year students the opportunity to remain in the early childhood setting in which they are employed. Students submit a detailed proposal stating their objectives with regard to a particular aspect of early childhood education practice. The proposal has to be approved by the course coordinator. In addition, they nominate a mentor to guide them through the practicum. During the practicum, students complete a reflective journal and submit it, together with the assessment documents, at the end of the practicum.

The three practicum options reflect a desire to offer a choice to students and to meet the objectives of the program within contexts suited to the individual circumstances of the students. The benefits of offering students choices while they prepare to become early childhood professionals include students' willingness to experiment with their classroom practices in an atmosphere characterized by trust (Richardson 1990).

Benefits of the practicum

A great deal of debate has taken place regarding the role that field experience plays in teacher development and the relative contributions of various individuals and institutional factors to the socialization of new teachers (Zeichner 1985). The practicum experience comprises a complex set of relationships among program features, settings, and people (Hersh, Hull, & Leighton, cited in Zeichner 1985, 44). The Option C practicum is no less complex than Option B, even though it is carried out in the student's own workplace. Relationships between students and their colleagues, mentors, university supervisors, and university practicum administrator—all influence the experience.

Field experiences have been found to benefit all participants (e.g., Jones 1993). While those involved have recognized that the process is time-consuming, they have also realized that the benefits are significant and thus

worth more than the initial investment. Jones talks about the fact that this may be considered the "longer way around" but states that the rewards are evident in teacher growth in terms of competency and "the energy that comes from intrinsic motivation" (Jones 1993, 147). Jones recognizes that "tapping into the energy of self-directed learning is crucial in promoting quality in schooling and child care" (p. 147). This is clear in the Option C program, in which the mentor is the mainstay for the student in making links between the practicum and early childhood philosophies and practices.

The university supervisor acts as a liaison between the student and the supervising teacher or mentor. Because each practicum context is unique, there is a need to interpret the requirements, as set out in the course aims and objectives, in relation to the individual characteristics of the site. Should problems arise, the university supervisor acts as negotiator, problem solver, or counselor for both the student and the supervising teacher. The latter two have a strong working knowledge of the daily progress made, and the university supervisor acts as a catalyst to ensure that they discuss and evaluate issues as they arise. Practically, the university supervisor initiates contact with the student prior to the commencement of the practicum and makes one visit, as close to the midpoint of the practicum as possible during the two-week period. The practicum administrator maintains a database that, together with her or his personal knowledge, makes for an effective match of supervisors and students in widespread geographical locations and early childhood settings.

Feedback from students and their employers indicates that the practicum experience is a valuable constituent of the course. The two practicum units not only link theory with practice, but they also afford a prime opportunity for students to interact with others in the course and build networks within the early childhood profession. Notes and readings are sent to students prior to the field study to guide their planning and complement the other units that make up the course. Each student is required to contact the practicum administrator in order to determine placement for the period. Such contact, which is an essential part of monitoring the quality of the practicum experience, is supported by the extensive network of early childhood educators built up since the course was begun.

Learning from field experience through narratives

The use of narrative, also called *storytelling*, as a teaching tool is, of course, not a new idea in education (Egan 1988), and the concept has been used in areas such as artificial intelligence to develop software that supports "Aesopic teaching" (Ferguson et al. 1992). In particular, storytelling recognizes the significance of a community of practitioners as the source of what is important to know, do, and talk about.

Sharing student experiences

The practice of students sharing stories from their practicum experiences was spurred by the desire to have students learn from each other's experiences in a meaningful and relevant manner. The stories provide insights into teachers' practices and benefit all who listen to them (Witherell & Noddings 1991; Ferguson et al. 1992; Weber 1993).

Apart from sustaining a sense of sharing and participation among the students, the stories foster a communal feeling of their having a lot in common. Moreover, as Genishi (1992) said,

> Stories allow us to generalize to our own experiences, to see ourselves in new scenes or scenes similar to those we know, such as other's classrooms. We can make comparisons between their theories, decisions, and behaviors and our own; and we can imagine changes, new directions in plots, different scenes or endings in our classroom stories. (p. 201)

Students share narratives in teleconference sessions and study school sessions. Study schools are optional sessions offered each semester. They provide opportunities to discuss issues and interact with peers in a semistructured context. Attendance at these sessions, which are conducted on weekends, is high. Feedback from students has indicated that many consider the sessions to be valuable because they feel isolated when studying in external mode.

Narratives, reflection, and change

The practicum experience is multidimensional, and the narratives shared often capture the richness, indeterminacy, and complexity of teaching. Carter (1993) states that stories allow teaching events to be framed in the context of a teacher's life history; they represent a way of knowing and thinking that often brings to light issues arising in the practicum. Kelchtermans and Vandenberghe (1994) and Knowles (1993) emphasize that teaching principles are embedded in narratives and legitimized with concrete experiences.

The collection of students' stories from a practicum yields many interesting insights. For students, reading the stories stimulates thinking that is vital to change, while for teacher educators, the stories provide valuable feedback about the effectiveness of the practicum. Clandinin (1992) and Connelly and Clandinin (1990) suggest that teachers' personal narratives help them to reflect on their pedagogy in relation to specific contexts and this process then extends their personal knowledge about the practice of teaching. In teachers' narratives, not only is cognitive knowledge about teaching validated, but the emotional aspect of storytelling reinforces the feeling of effectiveness and competence, thereby enhancing teachers' job satisfaction (Kelchtermans & Vandenberghe 1994).

Change is often regarded as difficult for teachers to accept (Richardson 1990), and it has been suggested that teachers particularly resist complex, conceptual, longitudinal changes. For some of the teachers in training in the program, the change from teaching in secondary and primary schools to teaching young children is quite dramatic. Richardson (1990) has suggested that, to effect worthwhile and significant change, it is necessary to embed practice within theory. Toward this end, we believe that teachers need to have opportunities to share, talk about, and reflect on their experiences. The choice of practicum—particularly Options A or C—allows for such opportunities.

Making sense of stories recounted in the practicum

Using the narrative methodology presupposes that the storyteller sets the agenda and that the story is a subjective interpretation of the facts (Carter 1993; Clift 1994; Kelchtermans & Vandenberghe 1994). Accordingly, the practice will likely empower early childhood educators, who have a wealth of stories to tell about child-centered practices.

We have collected stories from phases ranging from the practicum planning through the submission of the reflective journal and the practicum evaluation form. The contexts are varied and include

- face-to-face interviews and phone conversations (between student and administrator, course coordinator, colleagues, and mentor prior to the submission of the practicum proposal),
- teleconferences and study schools,
- submissions of the practicum proposal for approval,
- journals (those kept by students during their practicum and those kept by practicum administrators).

The stories collected from students thus far reveal that the following issues are of basic, critical importance to early childhood educators:

- the physical, professional, and social *features* of the practicum and how they affect each student's experience;

- how a student's personal narrative influenced his or her *motivation* to undertake the requirements of the practicum;
- how the students *viewed* the practicum and themselves within the early childhood setting;
- features of the practicum the students deemed *useful and appropriate* and those they deemed *detrimental* to their development as early childhood teachers.

Practicum experiences through student eyes

The students' narratives reflected their experiences with the practicum they selected. Although there was considerable overlap in the fieldwork experiences, the stories highlight the benefits unique to each practicum and the ways in which the option's format facilitated learning about teaching young children.

Stories from Option A, the school holiday program

In this practicum option, classes take place in a registered early childhood center during the university vacation period. A qualified, experienced early childhood educator coordinates the classes and guides the students in a variety of ways. The children attending the program are drawn mainly from the community in which the center is located.

The stories presented with regard to this option reflected a number of recurrent themes:

- the significance *of working as a team*, which supports the sharing of ideas about the creation and development of curricula and skills for teaching young children;
- the nature of the *support* shown by colleagues and the supervising teacher;
- increased levels of *confidence* in teaching resulting from the communal effort of all participants;
- the *growth* in personal, language, and communication skills;

• a sense of *ownership* of the program and empowerment arising from the effective planning and implementation of ideas;

• a recognition of the importance of *sharing ownership* with the children so that they can become effective learners and thinkers.

Ellen had intended originally to fulfill her practicum requirement at the local child care center in a country town prior to Christmas. When the supervising teacher resigned suddenly, Ellen was forced to reschedule her annual family vacation so that she could participate in the school holiday program. This actually was a fortuitous event for Ellen, who said that the shared experience of the program was a valuable learning opportunity for her and clearly had had an impact on her later development as a teacher.

Ellen: I've gotten a lot more out of just talking to people. The best part has been sharing ideas and seeing other people teach or model, including the supervising teacher, who had so many resources. We formed two teams that worked together really well. The two [students] that I worked with were infants trained, whereas the other [students] were home science teachers. We understood each other's "lingo." We took leads from each other and were able to jump in when we saw a chance.

Annabel chose to enter the school holiday program because she felt that working with a group of students would help her gain more confidence in handling new experiences than if she were on her own.

Annabel: It was a wonderful experience as we supported each other. I had never worked in a group before and I felt very hesitant. However, my experiences in the two-week practicum with group collaboration gave me confidence. It was gratifying knowing that you could get support from colleagues in a setting where many ideas and challenges can be tried out. It improved my communication skills.

Brenda decided to enroll in the school vacation program because she had heard from a previous student that it was a valuable experience. Her narrative highlights what she felt were the advantages for her and her colleagues.

Brenda: We had ownership of a program with ample resources and an ideal setting. During the practicum, personal relationship skills of negotiation and respect for others were developed. Individuals could share areas of expertise and be supported in areas of weakness. We had ample time for group collaboration, which was supported by open and effective communication.

I loved seeing the children take control of their learning and build on an idea or activity, producing a very authentic learning experience.

Natalie chose the program reluctantly. She didn't want to lose two weeks' pay, and the director at her center didn't want her to be away from her group at the time. After numerous phone calls, it was resolved that Natalie could participate at the university's Toddlers Center. Like Ellen, she described the shared experiences that were most valuable to her.

Natalie: I've really enjoyed it. I've learn[ed] so much about planning. When I got my job, I had no early childhood background, and there was not a great deal of support from my colleagues. I feel more confident about planning and observing the children. It's been good to hear other people's point of view—how other people have interpreted things differently from how I interpreted things and different ideas on how to follow up on things that we observed.

These stories highlight the value of the school vacation program as a practicum for graduate students. The shared experiences in planning and in interacting with the children were identified as aspects that not only made students more confident, but also helped them develop a sense of what it meant to be an early childhood teacher.

Stories from Option B, the individual practicum

Option B allows the students themselves to seek placement in a practicum, usually in their locale. The students submit an application to the practicum administrator for approval to enter the program and to be assigned a university supervisor. Personal commitments, such as family obligations and employment situations, are a major influence on the type of setting that is chosen.

The majority of students choose Option B for their second and final practicum, after having enrolled in a school holiday program. The narratives coming out of this option reveal a recognition of the significance of the change of context from a team situation to an individual situation and a realization of the critical influence of the supervising teacher on the experience.

It is interesting to note a shift in the focus of the stories, which now center on the following features:

• the *skill* of the supervising teachers and their ability to *model* effective practice,

• the *hierarchical* nature of the relationship between the student and the supervising teacher,

• a willingness on the part of the student to *explore* new contexts for learning with children in a *different age group* from those taught previously,

• a comparison of contexts for teaching and learning based on *personal experiences*.

Dana had participated in a school vacation program and then completed an individual practicum. It was apparent that she felt that her first experience in the collaborative setting was more valuable than working with just one other teacher. She recounted,

Dana: It was good to see how others did things and then to be able to talk about it in the school [vacation] program. . . . I really believe that teachers learn best from watching other teachers, and I really missed that on my second [practicum]. The local preschool teacher was also studying and encouraged me to work with her. I missed the camaraderie of the first [practicum], plus the fact that I left [it] with lots of ideas ready to try, and after the second [practicum], I felt that [the local teacher] learned more from me than I did from her.

Janet had been a high school teacher for 12 years when she decided that she wanted to change the focus of her teaching career. Her story exemplifies some of the problems associated with students working with caregivers with completely different styles and philosophies. It also reveals the role of the reflective journal as a means of sharing problems when oral communication is difficult.

Janet: I did the [vacation] program first. . . . By the second [practicum], I wanted to do something different—to work with babies. I had trouble getting in, as the teachers were naturally very protective of their babies. There were two very different group leaders. . . . The thing that got me was the tension about how things should operate. There was [an] older woman who was about 60 and of the old school, very regimented. The other [caregiver] was in touch with the parents and very nurturing. It was cleansing and care versus play and activity. I was like the second teacher; I know that cleansing and care are important, but I wanted the children to be extended through play.

The university supervisor came when the [older caregiver] was on, so I could not tell her. So I wrote it in the journal and she read it instead.

Laura enrolled in the program to gain an early childhood qualification after teaching for some time a preschool group in a child care setting. Both of her practica were taken under Option B, and she mentions the differences that she observed in each early childhood setting.

Laura: I did my first [practicum] in child care and my second . . . in a state preschool. I liked the teacher and we had a good relationship. We shared a lot and it was really good from a professional development perspective. I felt that there were different management techniques in the two different contexts. The teachers in the preschool seemed to be more relaxed than those in the child care center. I think this meant that the children were more relaxed. I am not sure why. . . . The state schools have the backup from the education department, whereas the child care [center doesn't].

A story from Option C, the special circumstances practicum

Option C enables participants to remain in their own work settings. The student submits a proposal focusing on a particular aspect of the curriculum. After the proposal is approved, the student is assigned a mentor and a university supervisor for the practicum.

Option C represents a significant shift away from the team approach of the school holiday program and the approach in Option B, working with an experienced early childhood educator. Under Option C, the student is basically responsible for his or her own learning, and the role of the on-site mentor assumes increased importance. The university supervisor makes one visit, to ensure that the experience conforms to university and school standards.

The range of projects is broad, including

• creating learning centers,

• increasing parental involvement in the program,

• initiating an environmental education project,

• setting up a gardening plot,

• developing a program to facilitate the transition from home to school.

In the story that follows, it is evident that the chosen focus was quite innovative and the practicum represented the culmination of the course of study whereby the student was able to put into practice many of the principles she learned. By this stage of their growth, students

are able to synthesize all the elements of a successful learning program and realize the importance of becoming a reflective practitioner.

Kay completed her practicum in her first-year classroom. She wanted to offer the children in her class more choices in their learning environment through learning centers, so she phoned the practicum administrator, Jenny, for advice.

Jenny: Kay didn't have any particular ideas, but as the conversation continued, it appeared to me that her classroom didn't reflect many of the early childhood practices promoted in the course. I suggested that perhaps she could think about ways she could provide more choices for the children.

Kay: I wanted to broaden my teaching skills, knowledge, and understanding of the children by implementing learning centers into all curriculum areas. . . . If I was [in] a normal practicum, fear of failure would prevent me from trying such an idea with a new group of children in a short period of time. I believe that I will become a more proficient teacher and my children will display an increased interest in their learning as it becomes real and meaningful to them.

Jenny: Kay needed affirmation that she was going to succeed. She described the negative [feedback] she was getting from her teaching partner. At the end of the first week, Kay rang to say that the classroom was very busy, but that things were working well.

At the end of the practicum, Kay wrote,

Kay: At the time of my [practicum], my teaching partner wouldn't have [any] of it. But now he has come in on it too. . . . It's just working fabulously.

I felt overjoyed when I saw the children develop at their own rates as they took responsibility for their learning. I am happy not only with the children's development, but with my own achievements. I feel over the last two weeks I have become a keen "kid watcher." I've become more attuned to the [children's] needs and interests and learn[ed] to be flexible so I can cater [to] each individual accordingly. Performing in front of peers is certainly a more daunting task than I first imagined, but it creates an added pressure for you to succeed and prove your worth. This practicum has greatly changed my teaching style and the future of those placed in my care.

Kay also commented on the role of the reflective journal in her practicum experience.

Kay: I actually had a hard time with my reflective journal because I wasn't used to doing one. I ended up combining my planning with my reflective journal, and I could see everything—my feelings and the things that had gone wrong. I also put in what I was going to cover the next day. I found it a stress release doing that. I found it beneficial—especially at the end of my [practicum], when I reread the whole thing and I could see how much I had learn[ed] that time.

My supervisor was terrific. She came a number of times to talk and give us books to read, and it was very much a learning experience.

Kay's story illustrates the way in which the Option C practicum afforded her the opportunity to initiate something novel—learning centers. Having a reason to do this was obviously a catalyst for change, but another important feature was the fact that she had support from two experienced early childhood education professionals and was able to reflect on the process of learning and teaching.

Conclusion

This chapter has described the structure and organization of the graduate practica within the context of the Graduate Diploma in Education (Early Childhood) program. Ensuring quality and integrity in the program consisted of offering choices to our students in determining what sorts of practica were relevant to their needs and interests. In addition, students' journal narratives afforded a means of communicating information about the practica and constituted a medium for reflection by the students, which often acted as a powerful catalyst for change. Such student change, we believe, will manifest itself not only in alterations in behaviors and attitudes, but also in shifting philosophies of education.

The program was designed to give students different opportunities to experience the various contexts in which care and education are provided for young children. These contexts range from working on professional teams in the school holiday program, to working individually with an experienced early childhood educator, to working independently and taking responsibility for extending and reflecting on one's own teaching practices.

The structure of each of the three practicum options has evolved over time. The practica have been supported by our excellent university staff and an extensive network of exemplary early childhood education professionals, who have acted as supervisors and mentors for students.

The stories presented reveal that when students take on the responsibility for organizing their own practicum, they have a more valuable experience and, in turn, the children in their care profit. The stories focus on the organization and structure of the practicum from the students' perspectives. However, they also constitute a rich resource of information about many other aspects of the practicum, including the following:

• the "ecology" of the situation—context, interpersonal relationships, and planning during the field experience;

• the role of previous knowledge and experience;

• conditioned perceptions of the approach to the practicum;

• the role of the mentor and the university supervisor;

• the nature and use of the reflective journals;

• the role of critical reflection about one's teaching practice on policy and planning for young children in the context of the practicum.

The literature reports an increasing awareness of the use and importance of reflective practices in the preparation of staff for early childhood settings (e.g., Tertell, Klein, & Jewett 1998). In fact, in times of fiscal restraint, critical reflection is regarded as the most expedient way to enhance the quality of teacher education and, in turn, the quality of education offered to young children. Many teachers regard their work as solitary; therefore, the ability to reflect on their own practices can provide them with feedback that nurtures their self-esteem and professional growth.

More effective critical reflection occurs when an individual is able to engage in dialogue with other people. Thus, the role of the support staff is crucial. Smith (1997) suggests that a "critical friend is an impetus for powerful reflection" (p. 8).

Mentors and other supportive colleagues create a positive learning climate in which students are able to engage in discourse, debate, risk taking, and critical analyses that promote meaningful learning and empower them to become more effective early childhood education professionals.

References

Carter, K. 1993. The place of story in the study of teaching and teacher education. *Educational Researcher* 22 (1): 5–12, 18.

Clandinin, D.J. 1992. *Narrative and story in teacher education: Teachers and teaching*. London: Falmer.

Clift, R.T. 1994. Conversations with collaborators, colleagues, and friends: Representing others and presenting ourselves. *Educational Researcher* 23 (Aug.–Sept.): 29–31.

Connelly, F.M., & D.J. Clandinin. 1990. Stories of experience and narrative inquiry. *Educational Researcher* 19 (5): 2–14.

Darling-Hammond, L., ed. 1994. *Professional development schools: Schools for developing a profession*. New York: Teachers College Press.

Egan, K. 1988. *Teaching as storytelling: An alternative approach to teaching and curriculum in the elementary school*. London, ON: Althouse.

Ferguson, W., R. Bareiss, L. Birnbaum, & R. Osgood. 1992. ASK systems: An approach to the realization of story-based teachers. *International Journal of the Learning Sciences* 2: 95–134.

Genishi, C., ed. 1992. *Ways of assessing children and curriculum*. New York: Teachers College Press.

The Holmes Group. 1990. *Tomorrow's schools: Principles for the design of professional development schools*. East Lansing, MI: Author.

Jones, E., ed. 1993. *Growing teachers: Partnerships in staff development*. Washington, DC: NAEYC.

Kelchtermans, G., & R. Vandenberghe. 1994. Teachers' professional development: A biographical perspective. *Journal of Curriculum Studies* 26 (1): 45–62.

Knowles, J.G. 1993. Life-history accounts as mirrors: A practical avenue for the conceptualization of reflection in teacher education. In *Conceptualizing reflection in teacher education*, 70–92. London: Falmer.

Richardson, V. 1990. Significant and worthwhile change in teaching practice. *Educational Researcher* 19 (7): 10–18.

Smith, D. 1997. Facilitating reflective practice in student teachers. Paper presented at the third National Practical Experiences in Professional Education Conference, Adelaide, Australia.

Taylor, A. 1991. Recent Australian reports on teacher education: How far do they take us? In *Educating the educators: New directions in the recruitment and training of teachers*, Institute of Public Affairs, Education Policy Unit, 9–15. Canberra, ACT, Australia: Institute of Public Affairs.

Tertell, E.A., S.M. Klein, & J.L. Jewett, eds. 1998. *When teachers reflect: Journeys toward effective, inclusive practice*. Washington, DC: NAEYC.

Weber, S. 1993. The narrative anecdote in teacher education. *Journal of Education for Teaching* 19 (1): 71–82.

Witherell, C., & N. Noddings, eds. 1991. *Stories lives tell: Narrative and dialogue in education*. New York: Teachers College Press.

Zeichner, K.M. 1985. The ecology of field experience: Toward an understanding of the role of field experiences in teacher development. *Journal of Research and Development in Education* 18 (3): 44–51.

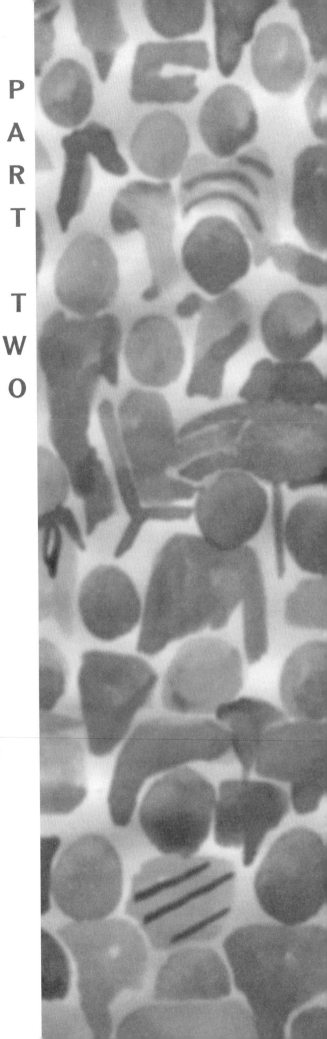

Developing Meaningful Learning Opportunities

Barbara Piscitelli

4

Practicing What We Preach: Active Learning in the Development of Early Childhood Professionals

"The values of discovery learning are as relevant at 33 as they are at 3.
—University student

The Very Hungry Caterpillar came to visit our city for three busy weeks in September one year. The university had an agreement to prepare and supervise a team of student teachers who would guide visitor learning in an exhibition of 50 of Eric Carle's original picture book illustrations. Taking on the job meant endless hours of work, but the results confirm that it is possible and highly desirable to involve university students in community-based projects as part of their professional development.

The real-world orientation of the project provided an opportunity to put into practice many of the theories early childhood educators espouse—that people learn by being involved in meaningful activity, that adults and children should learn together in specially designed environments, and that learning can take place outside of the classroom. Over the course of just 19 days, we met four thousand visitors age 6 months to 75 years and took them to look at The Art of Eric Carle, a specially designed interactive exhibition with an art gallery, a large model of a leaf on which storytelling took place, a puzzle nook, a chalkboard cavern, and an art studio for painting and decorating papers. The teacher education students who participated in the project reported that they learned how to work as a team to plan, implement, and evaluate a high-quality environment for children, teachers, parents, and grandparents.

This ambitious project illustrates the active-learning strategy that plays a large role in my teaching in both the university classroom and the community.

Active learning for adults

Active learning is as important in adult education as it is in early childhood education (Jones 1986). In two areas of early childhood professional development—visual arts education and ethical leadership—active learning has enabled my students to apply specific ideas and principles in workshop-based tutorials, problem-solving seminars, and community-based activities. The visual arts education classes present a wide range of activities: setting up children's art exhibitions in the local community, writing catalogues for children's art exchanges, participating in hands-on art sessions, and developing special museum–school projects. The ethical leadership classes explore a range of issues affecting children, particularly issues relating to their human rights. Students interview local advocates for children and report to the class about those individuals' achievements and personal qualities.

Key teaching strategies

Certain key teaching strategies seem to ignite students' interests, so that they get a rich understanding of the fundamental principles of working with, and on behalf of, children. Lectures address some central ideas in a structured format. A list of reference materials enables students to learn more about ideas touched on relatively briefly in the lectures. Formal meetings provide a platform to try out new ideas, convey results of current research, and discuss work in progress. Students enjoy the opportunity to sit and think, to gather ideas, and, through slides, videotapes, and other communication media, to examine how theory is put into practice.

Early childhood programs are most effective when they include workshops in which students have practical experiences—debating issues, gathering resources, collaborating on a project, and other such activities—that enable

Hands-on Experience— Involving Students in Community Arts Festivals

University students studying early childhood traditionally gain much of their background indoors, in the college classroom and as student teachers. However, teaching experience outside of a school setting is valuable as well. Direct involvement in community events such as children-focused festivals can provide the future educator with the kind of hands-on practice in experiential learning that no classroom exercise or university discussion could provide. Two such Australian events are the Barefoot in the Park festival for children under age 8 and the Out of the Box Festival of Early Childhood, designed for children ages 3 to 8.

The students involved in these two festivals were encouraged to participate as volunteers and were not formally assessed. However, they were required to keep reflective journals and to link their experiences to a practice teaching block. The students had a high degree of control and responsibility over their participation, and they selected subject matter as well as defined their own amount of involvement.

A range of benefits

Overall, the results of the students' involvement were very positive. The out-of-school context of the festival setting seemed to result in more effective planning; the students took greater control of what was offered to children and families because they were directly responsible for it.

Learning in a field setting engaged the students on a different level than in class: they were able to identify the value of creating a

—Cassandra Weddell

dynamic learning environment and responding to the various needs of individuals. Constant spontaneous and personal interaction with young children opened their eyes to more effective ways of relating to them. As one student reported in her journal, "I didn't realize just how powerful voice, eye contact, and gesture are. They capture children's imagination instantly."

The students also benefited from interaction with peers, professional artists, parents, and community volunteers. Working in a group context with other students provided the opportunity to plan and evaluate collectively, building group cohesion and support in the process. Interaction with families, professionals, and members of the community taught the students much about different techniques and approaches to dealing with children. This challenged and encouraged the students to articulate their own beliefs.

Conclusion

The festival is an ideal field site for students studying early childhood learning and development, and merits further study. Participating in these community-based events, which involve hundreds of thousands of children and their families each year, enables students to view children and families differently. Working with community-based performers and event organizers also broadens their view of alternatives to traditional employment as teachers.

In the end, however, it is the ability to interact with children in a nontraditional setting that contributes most valuably to the future educator's own education.

them to develop important skills. Sometimes, simulation or role playing takes the place of direct experiences that would be cumbersome or difficult to carry out.

Volunteering in the community

In considering the impact of active engagement on learning, many people naturally focus on young children and early childhood education. However, in the field of education, teachers at all levels and in all walks of life incorporate project-based and other active-learning approaches in their curriculum. For example, some involve their students in community arts festivals geared toward young children (see box). Across the adult education sphere of universities, colleges, and professional development, an extensive range and diversity of active-learning experiences emphasize problem-based learning, studio activities, and laboratory sessions. Increasingly, work experience and community volunteerism draw people into various occupations and professions.

Historical roots of active learning

Many leading researchers, philosophers, and early childhood educators have argued that people learn best through firsthand experiences.

John Dewey

Active-learning philosophy can be traced back to John Dewey (1859–1952), whose pragmatic philosophy and practical approach to learning were well known to society at large. Dewey lectured to thousands of people each year, his books and lectures were read widely around the world, and his views were popular in the early part of the twentieth century.

In 1897, Dewey published his manifesto on teaching, a document that set out his beliefs about education, schooling, the curriculum, and teaching methods. He stressed the importance of meaningful activity in the school as a means of finding a balance between the personal needs and interests of the individual and the formation and growth of a "proper social order" (Dewey 1897, 638). He also emphasized the importance of purposeful education in which learners and teachers actively work on communally developed projects (Dewey & Dewey 1915).

Maria Montessori

At the same time that Dewey was gaining prominence as an educator, Maria Montessori (1870–1952) stressed the importance of various teaching materials and interactive strategies in promoting learning in young children (Montessori 1948a, 1948b). She and her disciples demonstrated the Montessori method of education in classrooms in Europe, North America, and India. Her educational philosophy was based on a method of teaching that used a set of sensory apparatus designed to promote children's self-directed learning and development.

Other educators and researchers developed and adapted various projects and materials for the education of young children. Over the past hundred years, active-learning approaches have been promoted through books, articles, and formal degree courses taught at teachers colleges or universities, as well as in workshops and other professional development programs run by employers and professional associations.

During the twentieth century, the coursework of most specialized early childhood teacher education programs emphasized preparing early childhood educators for their work by actively experimenting with teaching methods and materials, by learning skills through observation, planning, and evaluation, and by forming views on various theories and philosophies of education. The legacy of Montessori and Dewey is still evident in early childhood teacher education programs, many of which focus on connecting theory with practice through real-life experiences (Cuffaro 1995).

Active learning in teacher education

Today's early childhood professional development programs stress various attitudes, skills, systems of knowledge, and dispositions to be adopted in working with children, families, and the larger community. Agreement is widespread regarding the importance of mentoring adult learners and challenging their intellectual and practical development in the process of becoming "good" teachers of young children (Yonemura 1986; Ayers 1989). In many college and university classrooms, this vision translates into a program with a dual emphasis on personal growth and professional development. The disposition, skills, and knowledge required to become a good teacher of young children are developed over time, in an active process of trial and error with opportunities for reflection and guidance provided within a supportive environment.

Jones (1993) sees this dual emphasis on personal growth and professional development as the key objective of a constructivist model of learning wherein adults (as well as children) learn through employing purposeful actions in their environments and engaging in meaningful interactions with other people. The model affords an important opportunity for the college or university staff to "practice what we preach" by bringing to life many of the tenets of our educational philosophies.

Tenets of active learning

The active-learning philosophy holds that learning

• is a process of engagement with resources and ideas,
• involves people solving problems and discovering new things,
• contributes to personal development and social change,
• occurs sometimes in isolation but more often in collaboration with others,
• ignites creativity.

Developing Meaningful Learning Opportunities

These progressive tenets are a rationale for active learning from the university to the kindergarten levels and are deeply embedded in the practices and philosophies of early childhood educators. Yet they are very difficult to implement, unless students attain a deep understanding of the nature and benefits of such an approach to teaching and learning.

One of the best ways of learning how to use active-learning approaches in an early childhood education environment is to have first-hand experience as an active learner; mere rhetoric will not result in active learning in the classroom. University and college teachers have a golden opportunity to put the tenets into practice through face-to-face contact with their students. In my work with adult learners, I employ those principles and discuss how to use the same approaches with young children and their families.

Active learning projects for adults

In working with adult learners preparing to be teachers of young children, one can employ a range of teaching to convey the basic philosophy of active learning. At the most explicit level, the instructor tells the students, "I believe in active learning and in learner-centered education." A critical step is to explore students' current knowledge and practical skills—only with some understanding of where the students are in their development can the teacher educator effectively proceed to work with them in thinking about how to achieve child-centered education. This approach requires challenging students' notion of the instructor or teacher as the center of the curriculum, in favor of establishing a range of hands-on, "minds-on" learning activities that allow them to select and work on their own projects (Jones 1986, 1993).

Visual arts activities

The tasks that prompt students to engage actively with ideas differ with the subject. For instance, some visual arts activities (e.g.,

drawing, painting, and three-dimensional construction) involve developing and representing ideas with various media and materials. For many students, this will be the first time they have used such materials to express ideas since their own childhood. The ways in which they approach the tools, the materials, and the task provide valuable information and a basis for discussion.

In documenting their intellectual development, the instructor learns more about the students and, further, may be able to use some of their ideas and questions to reflect on the bigger picture of teaching in early childhood classrooms. As students work, teachers interact with them, prompting them to discuss their ideas with each other and with the instructor, to use a different strategy, to try out a new solution to a problem, to look for other materials, or to show them how to use a tool (Jones 1993; Carter & Curtis 1994). The teacher also may take notes on students or photograph them engaging in various activities (Jones 1986).

Ethical leadership

Teaching about ethical leadership requires a variety of other strategies and resources that prompt a learner-centered, active-enquiry approach (e.g., Feeney, Freeman, & Moravcik 2000). In contemporary society, numerous issues affect the lives of teachers of young children. One way to set the stage for discussing such topics is to show students news clippings of a range of stories about local, national, and global issues affecting children. For example, students may scan newspapers for reports on child abuse and violations of children's rights in their own nation and in the world at large. The newspapers make these real-life issues and impress upon students the importance of being informed about current issues that affect children.

Ethical leadership requires informed practitioners. In the early stages of development, novices may learn best by working with experienced advocates. At the local level, students may research an issue of interest, either independently or in pairs, and then present their findings to the group in an environment characterized by open discussion and critical thinking. Often, the students find that they have to read up on current local legislation, study community attitudes, and develop a balanced position for dealing with such problems in their teaching career. Some students write letters to the editors of newspapers on laws, policies, and practices that they find unethical or demeaning to children.

For the most part, the students use their time to become increasingly articulate about issues that affect young children and learn how to deal with disturbing problems from an ethical and professional viewpoint. To this end, they use codes of ethics (AECA 1990; NAEYC 1998) to inform their decisions about how and when to act in children's best interests.

Criteria for successful active-learning projects for adults

Active-learning projects can be very exciting for both students and staff, but it is important to ensure that such projects have educational as well as pleasurable outcomes. In contemporary society, the push for achievable educational objectives sometimes focuses on academic pursuits without due consideration to the importance of affective goals.

In the professional development of early childhood teachers, the challenge is to balance the personal and practical knowledge of teaching with the knowledge bases of the various disciplines children may encounter in their early years. Active-learning projects may provide one means of balancing practical knowledge and theoretical knowledge if the university or college teacher takes time to deconstruct and evaluate the project with the students. This approach is in keeping with the view that people learn not simply by doing, but also by understanding the consequences of their actions (Cuffaro 1995).

Five key criteria can be used to guide the selection and organization of active-learning projects in teacher education programs.

• **Staff and students work together to develop and complete projects.** In an active-learning environment, staff may make some preliminary decisions about the nature of what is to be examined in the class. These initial plans and the reasons for them should be explained to the students; however, negotiation should be permitted, to ensure that the suggested activities are relevant and meaningful to the students. Decisions should be based on the needs of the group, the subject to be explored, and the relevance of the topics to the learners. This aspect of active learning puts the teacher and the student in the role of colearners and coconstructors of the curriculum. Negotiation demonstrates the importance of democratic decisionmaking and is a strategy that may be used successfully with children.

• **Staff provide time for students to discover ideas, solve problems, and complete their projects.** Students require adequate time to engage in projects. In a workshop session of two to three hours, the environment should be organized so that students have time to develop a plan, experiment with some ideas, and find a way of completing a task. Because it may be impossible to complete a project within such a short time span, the staff should discuss with students the best way to work on long-term projects and should make the workshop available to students outside of regularly scheduled sessions. Students will profit from learning how to set objectives that are achievable in a given period of time, particularly if they have had to do so as part of their education.

Staff should allocate adequate time for cleaning up at the end of a workshop session, as that is an important part of every teaching situation and involves learners in taking care of their resources, equipment, and shared space. Time should also be set aside to talk

Developing Meaningful Learning Opportunities

about the lessons learned in an active-learning environment. Sometimes students are reluctant to evaluate their own learning, but if the staff takes time to invite comments and listen to the responses, much can be discovered about learning styles, teaching problems, and broader educational issues.

• **Adequate resources are available to students.** We have designed two large active-learning labs to model the facilities available in most early childhood centers. Built to accommodate up to 30 students, each lab contains sinks, tables, stools, workbenches, and storage shelves. Kitchen appliances offer resources for both health and nutrition and for various other "cooking" activities. Small groups may work at large tables. Shelves can be stocked with a variety of open-ended resources, such as paper, paint, glue, fasteners, recycled materials, natural materials, and household items. Storage units house costumes, props for plays, and musical instruments. A carpeted space on the floor provides a spot for sitting and telling stories, presenting or watching plays, or improvising tunes.

Active-learning labs and the materials in them are valuable resources for teaching. Because many faculty members use lab space and resources over the course of a semester, an effective reservation system is essential. Teaching in the labs enables early childhood educators to practice what they preach by establishing a context for the students to engage in the same type of activities and use the same kind of materials that are presented to young learners.

• **Staff encourage and model a process of active engagement and reflective thought.** Active learning requires the teacher to employ a range of planning and teaching strategies and abilities: good organization, well-planned objectives, excellent time management techniques, carefully honed observational skills, and a disposition to reflect on the teaching–learning enterprise. Teaching staff who devise

plans together with their students will find a multitude of tasks to be undertaken and apportioned to the students, just as in project-based learning in early childhood classrooms. Once a project or activity has been selected, students and staff need to work purposefully to meet the objectives and learn from the experience. The activity may require ongoing adjustments to suit the resources and skills of the learners; negotiations should be undertaken to satisfy that objective.

Once a project or activity is under way, opportunities for reflection will arise. Staff and students should become aware of the ways in which their thinking is used to modify plans, renegotiate goals, work collaboratively, seek advice, locate resources, and manage the activity. Because thinking about one's own actions and thoughts—that is, metacognition—is central to the learning process, the instructor strives to make students more aware of their own thought processes and reasons for action. Heightened consciousness of their thinking in action is valuable to teachers as they manage their complex work in early childhood centers.

Reflection on one's teaching and learning is essential in the work of a skilled teacher (Tertell, Klein, & Jewett 1998). Students and faculty may benefit from taking time at each weekly meeting to discuss ideas that have emerged since the last class meeting. Either may read entries from personal journals or raise questions that need to be discussed. Keeping a weekly journal enables the instructor to stay focused on the needs, interests, and ideas of the students. Journal entries may include remarks about students, expectations about what might have been learned, and strategies for the next meeting.

• **Staff challenge students to work beyond their current knowledge base.** In keeping with learner-centered constructivist views, it is essential to encourage students to stretch their minds by continually working beyond their current knowledge base, so that they can grow intellectually, socially, and emotionally. Most students are excited by this challenge and willingly expand their repertoire of thoughts and actions. In the studio, tutorial or workshop environment, students can use role-play, simulation exercises, reflection, and invention activities to explore ideas. In a collaborative group, ideas are shared and elaborated by partners.

A small minority may dislike the active-learning process. Such students state that they prefer traditional lectures and set readings, and complain that workshops seem to have little purpose. This resistance to active learning may be the result of any number of factors. Sometimes, it is a fear of failure that leads students to resist the challenges of hands-on projects; other times, it may be their reluctance to join in with groups of learners (Belenky et al. 1986). Reluctant adult learners pose challenges to university teaching staff, and it is important to work alongside them to identify their resistance to the practical and social dimensions of active learning.

The benefits of active learning

Teacher educators and professional development teams find numerous benefits in using active-learning practices (Jones 1986, 1993; Carter & Curtis 1994). Students in such hands-on workshops and project-based environments testify to the intellectual, professional, and personal benefits of learning how to learn (Carter & Curtis 1994; Tertell, Klein, & Jewett 1998). The students gain a more secure and anchored understanding of the fundamental principles of early childhood education when they engage in active-learning approaches (Apelman 1993; Carter & Curtis 1994). Active learning presents a challenge to teacher-centered views of teaching, and students must find concrete ways of changing their practices to more learner-centered approaches. For example, having participated in an inservice course, one student reported,

The course consolidated my intuitive understanding of processes and procedures in early childhood [education]. These experiences supported a broadly based learning spectrum and, for me, enhanced the theoretical framework with practical linkages which were relevant, thought provoking, and sustaining. I realized that the early childhood principles of discovery learning are as relevant at 33 as they are at 3.

The professional benefits of active learning are numerous and varied. When teachers have a secure, anchored understanding of discovery-based active learning, they are in a position to support all who come to them to learn. Teachers who strive to understand the knowledge base of children, parents, colleagues, administrators, and politicians are in a better position to build positive interactions and two-way communication to extend each student's ability to learn (Bruner 1979; Yonemura 1986).

Students in preservice teacher education programs will benefit from learning how to justify, plan, and evaluate an active-learning program. Staff in elementary schools and early childhood programs will profit from ongoing inservice programs that renew their understanding of active learning and their organization of classes that promote it.

University staff may act as a catalyst for prompting a dialogue by encouraging preservice and inservice students to review their ideas and develop a strong statement of the core values that shape their thinking and actions in an active-learning classroom. Students could, first of all, develop their own list of key ideas and then support, extend, or challenge these intuitive concepts with further reading. For example, Jones (1993) and Carter and Curtis (1994) provide reading lists to stimulate discussions, and Bruner (1979) clarifies the benefits of intuitive understanding for ongoing learning.

At a personal level, too, teacher educators as well as students profit from an active-learning approach. The effort required to teach is far greater than with the conventional university teaching methods, but the rewards from investing in this personalized, humanistic approach to teaching are great (Carter & Curtis 1994). Not only is the approach of active learning congruent with the current philosophy of early childhood education, but it is also a lot of fun.

When staff and students meet face to face in a real-life workshop session, there is no set script to follow and no outcome that may be conclusively predicted. Thus, the nature of the educational enterprise in the university classroom mirrors the issues and problems faced by teachers of young children. There will be stumbling blocks, frustrations, elation, and sheer delight in any session, as students and staff probe issues, represent ideas, and solve problems. As teacher educators, my colleagues and I find this unpredictable setting invigorating and personally challenging.

A final word

When the Very Hungry Caterpillar inched out of town after three work-filled weeks, the student teams that were involved in the project took time to review what they had learned. Like many who have been involved in project-based learning (Katz & Chard 1989), they reported a total engagement with their learning and a thorough absorption with fostering the learning of others.

From the outset, these students were involved in choosing the ways in which the project would be conducted. They selected the project's objectives, developed the visitor schedule, worked out the roster, set up the exhibition and studio activities, and shared ideas with one another about how best to work with the visitors. As a result, they had a true sense of ownership over their learning environment and a feeling that they had each played a small, but vital, part in building the project.

These benefits and outcomes can be a part of all teacher education and professional development programs if educators take the time to build a collaborative, active-learning-based approach to their teaching and if there is a genuine regard for the ways in which people learn.

References

AECA. 1990. *Code of ethics.* Canberra, Australia: Australian Early Childhood Association.

Apelman, M. 1993. Co-creating primary curriculum: Boulder Valley schools. In *Growing teachers: Partners in staff development,* ed. B. Jones. Washington, DC: NAEYC.

Ayers, W. 1989. *The good preschool teacher: Six teachers reflect on their lives.* New York: Teachers College Press.

Belenky, M.F., B. Clinchy, N. Goldberger, & J. Tarule. 1986. *Women's ways of knowing: The development of self, voice, and mind.* New York: Basic.

Bruner, J. 1979. *On knowing: Essays for the left hand.* Cambridge, MA: Harvard University Press.

Carter, M., & D. Curtis. 1994. *Training teachers: A harvest of theory and practice.* St. Paul, MN: Redleaf.

Cuffaro, H. 1995. *Experimenting with the world: John Dewey and the early childhood classroom.* New York: Teachers College Press.

Dewey, J. 1897. My pedagogic creed. In *Three thousand years of educational wisdom: Selections from great documents,* ed. R. Ulich. Cambridge, MA: Harvard University Press.

Dewey, J., & E. Dewey. 1915. *Schools of tomorrow.* New York: EP Dutton.

Feeney, S., N. Freeman, & E. Moravcik. 2000. *Teaching the NAEYC Code of Ethical Conduct: Activity sourcebook.* Washington, DC: NAEYC.

Jones, E. 1986. *Teaching adults: An active learning approach.* Washington: NAEYC.

Jones, E., ed. 1993. *Growing teachers: Partners in staff development.* Washington, DC: NAEYC.

Katz, L.G., & S.C. Chard. 1989. *Engaging children's minds: The project approach.* Norwood, NJ: Ablex.

Montessori, M. [1948a] 1996. *The discovery of the child.* New York: Ballantine.

Montessori, M. 1948b. *To educate the human potential.* Madras, India: Vasanta.

NAEYC. 1998. *Code of ethical conduct and statement of commitment.* Washington, DC: Author.

Tertell, E.A., S.M. Klein, & J.L. Jewett. 1998. *When teachers reflect: Journeys toward effective, inclusive practice.* Washington: NAEYC.

Yonemura, M. 1986. *A teacher at work: Professional development and the early childhood teacher.* New York: Teachers College Press.

Carmel Diezmann and Nicola J. Yelland

5

Developing Mathematical Literacy in the Early Childhood Years

The importance of developing a mathematically literate populace who can function effectively with the practical mathematical demands of everyday life in the twenty-first century is recognized worldwide (e.g., Australian Council for Educational Research 1990; Her Majesty's Inspectorate 1998; Department of Education Training and Youth Affairs [DETYA] 1999; National Council of Teachers of Mathematics [NCTM] 2000). Mathematical literacy, also referred to as *numeracy,* pertains to the knowledge and skills that people need to participate effectively in mathematical situations relevant to their lives (e.g., DETYA 1999). In this chapter we use the term *mathematical literacy* rather than numeracy, because conceptualizations of numeracy are often restricted to number knowledge and skills, while mathematical literacy comprises the broad range of knowledge in number, measurement, space, chance and data, and skill needed daily for creative mathematical problem solving.

Educators generally face two challenges in helping children become mathematically literate. The first challenge is the widespread belief that mathematical literacy is not as important as verbal or written literacy (NCTM 2000); the second, the limited practical guidelines available for teachers attempting to impart a vision of mathematical literacy in our schools today (Pugalee 1999).

In this chapter we will discuss the importance of mathematical literacy in the early childhood years and present a model that serves as a framework for supporting young children's mathematical learning and development. We will also discuss educating early childhood teachers in math and promoting of children's math learning. In our program we provide students with many practical examples and strategies for helping young children explore and develop mathematic concepts in an environment characterized by active learning, inquiry, and problem solving.

The importance of mathematical literacy

The past decade has seen both huge advances in technology and a society surging to embrace technology. Each of these trends has had an impact on the development of skills and, in particular, mathematical literacy. In the precalculator era, people needed good arithmetic skills. Today, however, we have calculators and computers, and arithmetic skills alone are insufficient for understanding the vast amounts of data that we encounter. Everyday mathematical data now include graphs of home-loan payment options or tables comparing the charges of various telecommunication providers.

While people in the industrial age particularly needed to be *arithmetically literate*—performing quick calculations by hand—in the information age mathematical literacy must include being *data literate*. Although we still need basic computation skills, the emphasis has shifted to reading data and interpreting data effectively to discover trends, make predictions, and evaluate options. Machines conduct many of the routine calculations; people interpret, use and apply the results in their daily lives. In fact, Steen (1997) argued that being mathematically illiterate is a particular cause for concern in our "data-drenched" technological society:

> As information becomes even more quantitative and as society relies increasingly on computers and the data they produce, an innumerate citizen of today is as vulnerable as the illiterate peasant in Gutenberg's time. (p. xv)

While the importance of mathematical literacy has been acknowledged, it is often not seen as a priority for all students. Low societal expectations for mathematical literacy result in a practical outcome opposite to that envisioned for a mathematically literate society (Damarin 2000):

> Mathematics teachers and researchers have observed that mathematics is unique among school subjects in that, for many students, failure in mathematics is not an occasion of embarrassment: these students (often with the support of parents, peers, and sometimes guidance counselors and other teachers) refer to the inability to do mathematics with a certain pride. (pp. 8, 14)

Given this status quo, the achievement of mathematical literacy for all requires a proactive stance.

Foundations of mathematical literacy

Attaining mathematical literacy is a lifelong quest in an evolving technological society. However, children from birth to age 8 require particular attention in developing the foundations of mathematical literacy because during these years children undergo unparalleled cognitive, social, and emotional growth (Anning & Edwards 1999; NCTM 2000).

Children encounter mathematical ideas long before they attend school (Baroody & Wilkins 1999; Greenes 1999; Hunting 1999). For example, young children learn that money has value when adults take them along shopping, and they learn that birthdays occur at particular times of the year when they celebrate family birthdays. Real-life experiences are complemented by play experiences in which children assume the roles of shopkeepers and customers or "cook" cakes for a birthday party.

Young children generally participate in real-life or play experiences in the company of family, peers, or caregivers. Hence, adults and peers can support young children's learning. For example, parents support children's learning about number when they tell number-oriented stories, such as "The Three Bears." Older siblings may assist in developing an understanding of division when they share a packet of sweets, repeating "One for me, one for you."

While family members and others may provide intuitive support for children's mathematical learning, it is essential for early childhood educators to have a heightened understanding of how they can proactively support the development of the foundations of mathematical literacy.

Model for mathematical literacy

To give teachers guidance that enables them to contribute to children's mathematical literacy, Pugalee (1999) proposed a model consistent with NCTM's *Principles and Standards* (2000). The model identifies two key components of mathematical literacy—interrelated *processes* that are fundamental to doing mathematics and *enablers* that facilitate the doing of mathematics. In our teaching we regard the enablers as catalysts for mathematical literacy and have developed activities around them so that preservice teacher education students have the opportunity to explore ways to create rich mathematical learning contexts for young children.

Processes for mathematical literacy

According to Pugalee (1999), the processes of mathematical literacy incorporate

1. using *representation* as a building block for mathematical inquiry;

2. performing mathematical *manipulations*, such as calculations, algorithms, and procedures, in manual and technological situations (i.e., calculator, computer);

3. focusing on sense making in mathematical *reasoning* and using facts, properties, and relationships to make and test conjectures and follow and develop logical arguments;

4. *problem solving* by using prior knowledge and skills to reach and validate a solution, and posing one's own problems.

These processes are multifaceted and interrelated, and their use varies according to the experience and expertise of the child. Young children need to develop proficiency in each of these processes to participate in everyday mathematical situations (e.g., paying bus fare) and build a sound foundation for future mathematical learning.

Because the processes of mathematical literacy, as well as ideas for their development with young children, are detailed elsewhere (Copley 1999, 2000; Pugalee 1999; Yelland, Butler, & Diezmann 1999; NCTM 2000) our discussion highlights the key issues in early childhood teacher education related to each process.

Representing

Representation has long been recognized as critical for mathematical literacy. Children need to develop understandings of the various systems of representation, as shown in "Mathematical Representational Systems" (see p. 50). In this figure, real-world contexts are positioned at the center of the diagram to indicate their importance as key referents for each of the other representational systems.

Three key issues related to young children's understanding of representation are relevant to the development of the foundations for mathematical literacy.

Mathematical Representational Systems

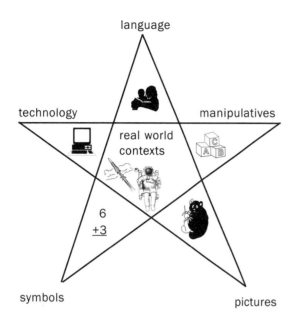

Source: Adapted by permission, from N.J. Yelland, D. Butler, & C. Diezmann, *Early Mathematical Explorations* (Needham Heights, MA: Pearson Custom Publishing, 1999).

Technology. While real-world experiences, manipulatives, pictures, language, and symbols are widely accepted mathematical representations (Lesh, Post, & Behr 1987), we feel that *technology* is also an important and unique representational system. For example, through technology young children can create, explore, and play in virtual worlds in dynamic ways that draw on and enhance spatial sense and other domains of mathematical knowledge and thought (e.g., Clements 1999a, 1999b; Yelland 1999).

Links. Helping children make *links* between different types of representations is key. Consider the number of everyday situations that depend on the rapid translation between representational systems. For example, we translate the symbolic into the concrete unconsciously and instantaneously when we see the price of a drink on a label and then pay for the drink with coins, which are tangible objects.

Clearly, there is everyday mathematical value in providing opportunities for children to translate between representational systems in the early childhood years.

Furthermore, developing the ability to translate between representational systems also provides a foundation for future mathematical situations. For example, illustrating the main characters of a story provides a base for later diagrammatic representation of the key elements of a problem—a task that many children find difficult (Dreyfus & Eisenberg 1990).

Systems. Individual differences in the use of representations need to be balanced by the use of various *representational systems* in mathematics. Individuals' preferences for particular representational systems for thinking and communicating are attributable, at least in part, to their unique profiles of intelligence (Gardner 1983). For instance, one child may be comfortable using a form of spatial representation, while another uses words to work through or explain the same problem.

In the early years, children's preferences may also be due to their limited experiences with some representational systems. Because a variety of representational systems are commonly used in mathematics (as shown in the figure on this page), children need to develop a certain level of proficiency with each system. Thus, teachers need to provide young children with rich experiences in all of the representational systems and also encourage children to develop their skills in their less preferred systems.

The mathematically literate person is one who can function effectively within a range of representational systems, including technology, and translate mathematical ideas from one system to another. Thus early childhood teachers need to address technology and translation and consider children's individual differences when planning and implementing learning opportunities for young children.

Developing Meaningful Learning Opportunities

Manipulating

Manipulating is closely associated with representation because manipulating involves the use of an object or symbol (i.e., representation). Two issues associated with the development of young children's manipulative ability require particular attention.

Materials. The manipulation of materials should be considered as relative to the child's level of understanding. While the use of materials can enhance children's mathematical understanding, their overuse can have a deleterious effect (Marjoram 1992):

> The child who already possesses the ability to add, subtract and multiply in his head can be positively bewildered by being made to perform the operation through his senses—with objects, coloured sticks and blocks. One may as well issue the football team with crutches. (p. 41)

Computers. Computer manipulatives may offer some practical and pedagogical advantages over physical manipulatives. For example, more materials can easily be generated on the computer screen as needed. Additionally, computer manipulatives such as on-screen pattern blocks can snap into position and remain correctly positioned, unlike physical materials, which move when they are accidentally knocked (Clements 1999b).

Manipulating materials has become synonymous with early childhood mathematics, yet teachers need to reflect on the reasons why young children use manipulative materials and consider the relative benefits of physical versus computer-based manipulatives.

Reasoning

Reasoning is a fundamental process in mathematics. Young children's reasoning should focus on sense making, which involves drawing logical conclusions, explaining and justifying thinking, and using patterns and relationships to analyze mathematical situations (NCTM 2000).

Guessing games provide a useful context for reasoning because they often involve children in reflecting on and modifying their ideas. For example, in a game where children guess a mystery number between 1 and 10, a child's initial guess of 5 is appropriate. However after a further clue that the number is even, the child who initially guessed 5 needs to change his response. If the child's second guess is 6, he would again need to change the guess after the final clue that the number is 5 less than 7.

Younger children can play similar guessing games with animals. For example, in a game where children guess a mystery animal from a set of pictures, a child's initial guess—let's say "duck"—is random. However after a further clue that the animal has 4 legs, the child changes her response to fit the clue, and so on with additional clues.

Contemporary research has highlighted two issues related to reasoning for consideration by teachers of young children. First, there is a need to identify and address the constraints that may inhibit young children's reasoning. Constraints to young children's reasoning include their limited knowledge base and their developing metacognitive skills (Metz 1995). These constraints may be overcome in classrooms with the use of scaffolding techniques (Metz 1995).

Second, teachers need to create supportive environments for reasoning. In such learning environments, teachers encourage young children to readily offer, justify, and question ideas associated with heightened reasoning (Watters & Diezmann 1998).

Problem solving

The importance of problem solving has been continually emphasized in the past two decades (e.g., NCTM 1980, 1989, 2000). Contemporary mathematics curriculums are designed so that children can engage in posing problems and solving them from the first years of schooling (e.g., NCTM 2000). However, two issues require attention if we are to be successful in achieving mathematics education reform goals (NCTM 2000).

Problem posing. Problem posing needs to be considered in tandem with problem solving. Problem posing involves the creation of a new problem from a given situation or experience and may take place before, during, or after solving a problem (Silver 1994). Posing problems can enrich and extend children's understandings and skills in problem solving, and a sound problem-solving background is essential for successful problem posing (e.g., English 1997).

Problem posing is quite difficult for many children and they need explicit guidance. Teachers in the early grades can strengthen children's problem-posing skills by strategies such as encouraging them to modify simple problems represented on cards (see the examples below). The task is simply to alter one or more of the cards, thus creating a new problem but maintaining the same basic structure.

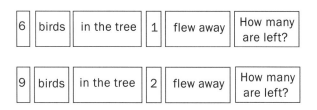

Investigations. Young children need opportunities to engage in mathematical investigations. A mathematical investigation can be characterized as a long-term, open-ended thematic exploration having multidimensional content and often embedded in a focus question (Brahier, Kelly, & Swihart 1999). For example, after we did some guided investigations involving M&M's candies, a group of 7- and 8-year-olds were encouraged to pose other questions about M&M's and investigate these problems.

One child decided to investigate something new—an M&M's cake. With the assistance of a parent, he baked different shape cakes to see what happened to the M&M's inside. He showed cut sections of different cakes to the group and explained that "You get the best rainbow effect inside the cake that has cooked the longest." His investigation focuses on how results varied with volume, time, and temperature.

Another boy commented on the difference in volumes, noting that before cooking, the cake batter took up about half the space in the cake pan, whereas the cooked cake filled the whole space. He also explained that the deepest cakes needed longer time to cook than the shallower cakes, even when the temperature was the same for all cakes. This investigation provided opportunities to integrate mathematics and science. This is viewed here as an integral part of early mathematical experiences.

Investigations are important for young children because they are authentic problem-solving situations in which children work as mathematicians and have opportunities to develop mathematical power (Baroody & Coslick 1998; Baroody 2000).

Our understanding of problem solving has evolved considerably since the early 1980s, and we need to continually evaluate the appropriateness of current problem-solving experiences for young children. Early childhood educators should consider both problem posing and mathematical investigations as important aspects of twenty-first century problem solving.

Catalysts for mathematical literacy

The processes of representing, manipulating, reasoning, and problem solving are not new to early childhood mathematics. However, an improved understanding of young children's learning and technological awareness has changed our conceptualizations of these processes and our expectations of young children in relation to them. In the this section, we discuss the catalysts used to promote the development of these processes.

Pugalee (1999) proposes that there are three catalysts in the development of these processes: communication, technology, and values. *Communication* enhances mathematical understanding, for example, through verbal interaction (e.g., Vygotsky 1978, 1987). *Technology* provides devices such as calculators and computers to enhance higher order thinking skills (e.g., Yelland 1999). *Values* highlight the importance of the affective domain (i.e., emotions, beliefs, attitudes) in learning mathematics (Renga & Dalla 1993).

Communication

Communication in social situations facilitates young children's learning through their interactions with each other or with knowledgable adults (Vygotsky 1978, 1987). In the early childhood years, much of such communication occurs during play. Play provides a rich social environment for learning (Berk 1994). For example:

• Children use drawing, construction, and other representational modes to explore and communicate ideas (e.g., creating a rocket out of blocks or shapes).

• As children explain and justify ideas to others, they refine and become more precise about them.

• Children talk through problems with one another, which helps them bring a problem to the conscious or metacognitive level. (For example, "We need to go this way because it's the shortest and uses less energy—it takes five steps and the other way is seven steps, which is more.")

Technology

Technology can provide young children with new mathematical environments and artifacts for problem solving, and it can stimulate learning. While the thoughtful use of technology has cognitive and motivational advantages, it re-

quires a reconceptualization of education, curriculum, and pedagogy (Yelland 1999). Educational applications of technology include computer software, the Internet, and computer-based manipulatives. Programs and materials vary in quality, education value, and purpose. For example, a program such as Tabletop (1995) allows children to represent data in various ways as well as manipulate them dynamically, and Shapes (1996) enables children to manipulate on-screen pattern blocks.

While software programs provide children with opportunities for interactive experiences with the processes of mathematical literacy, they should not be introduced randomly; programs should mesh with the curriculum and be carefully matched with a child's ability. Ensuring that young children are active learners and users of technology and incorporating technology into the curriculum are important (Wright & Shade 1994; NAEYC 1996).

Values

Values include beliefs and attitudes about mathematics that teachers hold and instill in young children. They are of particular importance in the development of mathematical literacy and can support or inhibit young children's learning (Renga & Dalla 1993). Examples of values that contribute to the development of children's ability to represent, reason, problem solve, and manipulate include

• appreciating that different ways of representating provide diverse and complementary ways of understanding a mathematical situation

• having the confidence to explain and justify ideas and critique others' ideas

• persevering to solve a problem

• believing that the use of manipulatives can lead to understanding

Clearly, communication, technology, and a sense of value about what we are doing assume an important role in enabling the development of mathematical literacy. Indeed, the role of these enablers as catalysts for learning extends beyond mathematics to all facets of early childhood teaching and learning.

Implementing the model: Educating early childhood teachers

Our work with preservice teacher education students has revealed that many of them need to develop their own mathematical literacy and review their attitudes toward mathematics before they embark on planning and implementing a program for the young children in their care. We have observed in students initial negative attitudes toward mathematics, as well as gaps in their knowledge of basic mathematical conceptual understandings. These observations were not surprising, given the perceived acceptability of mathematical illiteracy in the general community (Damarin 2000).

We have also noted, however, that when students are immersed in a learning environment characterized by active learning, inquiry, and problem solving, with ample opportunity to concentrate on the various aspects of the model of mathematical literacy described here, a distinct improvement occurs in their attitude toward mathematics and their conceptual understanding.

Knowledge and attitudes about mathematical literacy

Students' initial low levels of mathematical literacy may be due either to inadequacies in their formal education or to their falling behind in mathematics in a fast-changing world. While education plays a key role in the development of mathematical literacy, people also need to continually update their knowledge and skills to remain mathematically literate in this era of rapid technological change.

Adults update their mathematical knowledge and skills through acquiring new products (e.g., computers, cellular phones), using new services

---

Professional Development for Promoting Mathematical Literacy

Modeling

- Demonstrating hands-on math activities for students in class
- Using practica and other field experiences to enable students to observe skilled teachers engaging children in math experiences in the classroom
- Showing videos that illustrate the development of early mathematical literacy as it occurs naturally in everyday situations

Scaffolding

- Giving students the opportunity, individually or in groups, to modify or adapt a math activity for a younger age group after seeing older children do the activity
- Having students practice asking children good questions at particular points in a math activity (using videotaped segments of children working on math, for instance) before doing similar activities with children in the classroom
- Meeting with students frequently when they begin their practica and gradually meeting less often as they become more confident

Coaching

- Observing individual students as they work with children in small groups on a math activity and then discussing with them what worked and what did not.
- Employing peer coaching and mentoring strategies to give students constructive feedback on their teaching
- Involving students in creating practical resources for children's math learning and in giving one another feedback on these resources

Articulation

- Engaging students in critical discussion of readings about early math learning in which they summarize key ideas and formulate questions, linking the reading content to practical contexts

- Having students describe as precisely as possible a child's mathematical knowledge with respect to a specific problem (that is, what she appears to understand and not yet understand), based on a videotaped segment showing the child working on the problem and talking with a teacher about it

Reflection

- Engaging students in discussions about their observations, readings, and experiences, e.g., after a practicum visit, students discuss the teachers' attitudes toward math and how these were likely to affect children's attitudes

- Having students record in journals their classroom experiences with children and math, focusing on particular dimensions at different times (e.g., What did the children seek out and do spontaneously related to math, and how did this seem to affect their engagement? What did the student teacher's interaction with a child do to extend or intrude on the child's investigation or reasoning?)

Exploration

- Giving students a period of time to "mess about" with a set of math manipulatives to see what interesting discoveries and problems they might find

- Inviting students to explore math-oriented software to find out what can be done in a given program and discover ways of enticing children to investigate and represent mathematical ideas

(e.g., online banking), and capitalizing on new insights and opportunities in the economy (e.g., e-commerce). However updating is possible only when a solid foundation of mathematical knowledge and skills exists.

Negative attitudes toward mathematics can also have an impact on mathematical literacy. School experiences, unfortunately, seem to be a common source of such attitudes (e.g., Cornell 1999). Additionally, students may be concerned about their inability to use and understand technology. Comments such as "I don't understand computers" or "Computers scare me!" suggest a fear of the unknown that needs to be addressed in teacher education programs.

To address limited mathematical literacy or negative attitudes toward mathematics, our teacher education mathematics program has two further objectives:

- providing opportunities for the development of personal mathematical literacy, and

- engaging teacher education students in critical reflection about their attitudes toward mathematics.

Preservice teacher education students' inadequate knowledge base and inappropriate attitudes are not unique to mathematics. In Chapter 9, Grieshaber and Diezmann discuss how similar difficulties are successfully addressed with science teachers and in science teacher education programs.

Approaches to teacher education

Our teacher education program rests on the principles of cognitive apprenticeship, in which teacher educators support the students in their development of expertise in mathematics (Collins, Brown, & Newman 1989). Consistent with this approach, we look for opportunities to model effective teaching methods and interactions and to provide students with scaffolding and coaching wherever these may be helpful. We also encourage the students to articulate, reflect, and explore the multifaceted aspects of mathematical literacy.

In these efforts, we use a variety of strategies, as illustrated in the box, "Professional Development for Promoting Mathematical Literacy."

Students are able to further develop their expertise through reciprocal teaching in which they take turns assuming the roles of teacher and child (Palincsar & Brown 1984). Reciprocal teaching role play provides students with opportunities not only to practice the skills needed to support early mathematical literacy but also to develop their personal mathematical literacy skills.

In-class reciprocal teaching, however, often lacks the authenticity and complexity of an early childhood setting. To capitalize on the learning afforded by situated cognition (Brown, Collins, & Duguid 1989; Lave & Wenger 1991), we also provide opportunities for students to analyze noncommercial videos in which one of us assumed the role of a teacher of a group of young children. The use of video vignettes from an ongoing classroom-based research project allows students to explore some of the dilemmas currently faced by teachers and to elicit student suggestions about the ways we might be able to develop children's mathematical literacy. Because this project is current, there are also opportunities to provide students with feedback on the efficacy of their suggestions.

Thus, our model comprises a body of knowledge for the development of mathematical literacy, elements of apprenticeship, and socially shared intellectual work. These features have been identified by Resnick (1987) as critical in an effective program and are discussed by Yelland and Grieshaber in the Introduction of this volume.

Conclusion

Our future early childhood teachers will assume an important role in developing the foundations of mathematical literacy in young children for what should ultimately become a lifetime of mathematical learning. Mathematical literacy requires that teachers bring the outside (typical real-life situations requiring mathematics) into early childhood settings so that children learn to function mathematically in the everyday world. Teachers provide support for mathematical literacy development when they capitalize on spontaneous situations for mathematical learning, create rich situations for mathematical learning, and monitor children's mathematical learning.

Educators, however, also need to take the inside out—that is, take mathematics learning into the community. To do so, teachers need to maintain and develop their own mathematical literacy and become advocates for mathematical literacy in the wider community. Ways of maintaining one's mathematical literacy include participating in conferences and other professional activities of organizations such as the National Association for the Education of Young Children or the National Council of Teachers of Mathematics and reading professional books and journals. To mobilize teachers' ongoing professional development, instructors in our program inform students of local, national, and international resources they may find useful.

We hope that early childhood educators will develop skill in their interactions with children in meaningful and appropriate ways so as to foster the development of mathematical literacy and view it as an integral part of young children's experiences. In this way, teachers can give children opportunities to become active explorers of their environment, and mathematics will be a sense-making process with everyday relevance.

References

Anning, A., & A. Edwards. 1999. *Promoting children's learning from birth to five.* Buckingham, UK: Open University Press.

Australian Council for Educational Research. 1990. *Being numerate: What counts?* Victoria, Australia: Australian Council for Educational Research.

Baroody, A. 2000. Research in Review. Does mathematics instruction for 3- to 5-year olds really make sense? *Young Children* 55 (4): 66–77.

Baroody, A., & R.T. Coslick. 1998. *Fostering children's mathematical power: An investigative approach in K–8 mathematics instruction.* Mahwah, NJ: Erlbaum.

Baroody, A.J., & J.L.M Wilkins. 1999. The development of informal counting, number, and arithmetic skills and concepts. In *Mathematics in the early years,* ed. J.V. Copley, 48–65. Reston, VA: National Council of Teachers of Mathematics.

Berk, L.E. 1994. Vygotsky's theory: The importance of make-believe play. *Young Children* 50 (1): 30–39.

Brahier, D.J., M. Kelly, & J. Swihart. 1999. Investigations: This little piggy. *Teaching Children Mathematics* 5 (5): 274–80.

Brown, J.S., A. Collins, & P. Duguid. 1989. Situated cognition and the culture of learning. *Educational Researcher* 18 (1): 32–42.

Clements, D.H. 1999a. "Concrete" manipulatives, concrete ideas. *Contemporary Issues in Early Childhood* 1 (1): 45–60.

Clements, D.H. 1999b. The effective use of computers with young children. In *Mathematics in the early years,* ed. J.V. Copley, 119–28. Reston, VA: National Council of Teachers of Mathematics.

Collins, A., J.S. Brown, & S.E. Newman. 1989. Cognitive apprenticeship: Teaching the crafts of reading, writing, and mathematics. In *Knowing, learning and instruction: Essays in honor of Robert Glaser,* ed. L.B. Resnick, 453–94. Hillsdale, NJ: Erlbaum.

Copley, J.V., ed. 1999. *Mathematics in the early years.* Reston, VA: National Council of Teachers of Mathematics.

Copley, J.V. 2000. *The young child and mathematics.* Washington, DC: NAEYC.

Cornell, C. 1999. I hate math! I couldn't learn it, and I can't teach it!" *Childhood Education* 75 (4): 225–30.

Damarin, S. 2000. The mathematically able as a marked category. *Gender and Education* 12 (1): 69–85.

Department of Education Training and Youth Affairs. 1999. *The Adelaide declaration on national goals for schooling in the twenty-first century.* http://www.deet.gov.au/schools/adelaide/text.htm

Dreyfus, T., & T. Eisenberg. 1990. On difficulties with diagrams: Theoretical issues. In *Proceedings of the Annual Conference of the International Group for the Psychology of Mathematics Education Conference,* Vol. 1, eds. G. Booker, P. Cobb, & T.N. de Mendicuti. ERIC, ED 411137.

English, L.D. 1997. Promoting a problem-posing classroom. *Teaching Children Mathematics* 4 (3): 172–79.

Gardner, H. 1983. *Frames of mind: The theory of multiple intelligences.* New York: Basic.

Greenes, C. 1999. Ready to learn: Developing young children's mathematical powers. In *Mathematics in the early years,* ed. J.V. Copley, 39–47. Reston, VA: National Council of Teachers of Mathematics.

Her Majesty's Inspectorate. 1998. The National Numeracy Project. An HMI Evaluation. A report from the Office of Her Majesty's Chief Inspector of Schools. London, UK: Office for Standards in Education (OFSTED).

Hunting, R.P. 1999. Rational-number learning in the early years: What is possible? In *Mathematics in the early years,* ed. J.V. Copley, 80–87. Reston, VA: National Council of Teachers of Mathematics.

Lave, J., & E. Wenger. 1991. Situated learning: Legitimate peripheral participation. Cambridge, UK: Cambridge University Press.

Lesh, R., T. Post, & M. Behr. 1987. Representation and translation among representation in mathematics learning and problem solving. In *Representation in the teaching and learning of mathematics,* ed. C. Janvier, 33–40. Hillsdale, NJ: Erlbaum.

Majoram, D.T.E. 1992. Teaching able mathematicians. *Gifted Education International* 8 (10): 40–43.

Metz, K.E. 1995. Reassessment of developmental constraints on children's science instruction. *Review of Educational Research* 65: 93–127.

National Association for the Education of Young Children. 1996. NAEYC position statement: Technology and young children—Ages three through eight. *Young Children* 51 (6): 11–16.

National Council of Teachers of Mathematics. 1980. *An agenda for action: Recommendations for the 1980s.* Reston, VA: Author.

National Council of Teachers of Mathematics. 1989. *Curriculum and evaluation standards for school mathematics prepared by the working groups of the Commission on Standards for School Mathematics of the National Council of Teachers of Mathematics.* Reston, VA: Author.

National Council of Teachers of Mathematics. 2000. *Principles and standards for school mathematics.* Reston, VA: Author.

Palincsar, A.M., & A.L. Brown. 1984. Reciprocal teaching of comprehension-fostering and comprehension-monitoring activities. *Cognition and Instruction* 2: 117–75.

Pugalee, D.K. 1999. Constructing a model of mathematical literacy. *The Clearing House* 73 (1): 19–22.

Renga, S., & L. Dalla. 1993. Affect: A critical component of mathematical learning in early childhood. In *Research ideas for the classroom: Early childhood mathematics*, ed. R.J. Jensen, 22–39. Reston, VA: National Council of Teachers of Mathematics.

Resnick, L.B. 1987. Learning in school and out. *Educational Researcher* 16 (9): 13–20.

Shapes. [Computer software]. 1996. Palo Alto, CA: Dale Seymour Publications.

Silver, E.A. 1994. On mathematical problem posing. *For the Learning of Mathematics* 14 (1): 19–28.

Steen, L.A. 1997. *Why numbers count: Quantitative literacy for tomorrow's America.* New York, NY: The College Board.

Tabletop. [Computer software]. 1995. Cambridge, MA: Technical Education Research Centre (TERC).

Vygotsky, L.S. 1978. *Mind in society: The development of higher psychological processes.* Cambridge, UK: Cambridge University Press.

Vygotsky, L.S. 1987. *The collected works of L.S. Vygotsky,* eds. R.W. Rieber & A.S. Carton. New York: Plenum.

Watters, J.J., & C.M. Diezmann. 1998. "This is nothing like school": Discourse and the social environment as key components in learning science. *Early Childhood Development and Care* 140: 73–84.

Wright, J.L., & S.D. Shade, eds. 1994. *Young children: Active learners in a technological age.* Washington, DC: NAEYC.

Yelland, N.J. 1999. Reconceptualising schooling with technology for the twenty-first century: Images and reflections. *Information Technology in Childhood Education:* 39–59.

Yelland, N.J., D. Butler, & C. Diezmann. 1999. *Early mathematical explorations.* Needham Heights, MA: Pearson Custom Publishing.

6

Teaching Storytelling in Preservice and Professional Development Programs

Through play and narrative, children use their imaginations and creative thinking skills to understand their world; to synthesize, refine, and redefine their experiences; and to make links between past actions and future possibilities. Learning through playful encounters need not stop at kindergarten—adults, too, respond favorably to an approach to teaching and learning that encourages a sense of play.

This chapter discusses my own approach to teaching storytelling by considering the selection of resources to share, examine, and critique with students, the organization of classroom space and group work, the nature of workshop activities, and the stated expectation that all participants (including the instructor) will create a classroom environment based on mutual respect and support. These foundation stones of storytelling courses are realized in practical activities that reflect active participation, critical reflection, flexibility, and a respect for cultural diversity in the classroom.

Storytelling, teaching, and children's play

Storytelling and play, some would argue, are not the sort of things one ought to find in a school or university program. Especially with today's ever-pressing concerns for accountability, learning outcomes, and benchmarking in education, teachers and university lecturers are called upon more and more to justify their programs and to ensure that public money is well spent. Indeed, a survey conducted by Livo and Rietz (1986) on the status of storytelling in higher education in the United States led these authors to comment that

> Storytelling might be considered the Rodney Dangerfield of higher education. A depressing number of reactions [to the survey] implied that it "gets no respect.". . . Additionally, storytelling is misunderstood by academic scholars, as these responses illustrate: "Storytelling was dropped from the schedule to make room for

more 'academic' subjects." "We teach only secondary courses. Therefore, of course, there is no storytelling." (p. 446)

Although these misconceptions undermine the place of storytelling courses in universities, they may serve to strengthen instructors' resolve to provide storytelling courses that are theoretically sound and clearly relevant to classroom practice. Such courses may be offered across faculties of education, arts, and librarianship.

Despite any misgivings about the place of storytelling in university programs, storytelling, teaching, and play are inevitably fused together. Teaching, like storytelling, is a performance, and it shares many of the characteristics of storytelling in its use of voice, dress, movement, and gestures to convey meaning and engage the audience. Other features of storytelling (and teaching) convey a sense of play and playfulness. The storyteller (teacher) and the audience (students or children) recognize shared rituals and protocols and familiar story openings and closings, and they have expectations about what it means to be a storyteller and an audience. Perhaps most important is the way in which many teachers at all levels structure their lessons as exciting stories to be told.

Storytelling occupies a place in the play of children. Play is an important discursive practice of children and is frequently accompanied by story, song, movement, and gesture. Children's play often reaches into the realm of make-believe, where children improvise situations that arise from "ideas" (Vygotsky 1978). A similar perspective is offered by Britton (1992), who sees the transition from the real world to the world of fantasy as a transition from "the world of objects to the inner world of ideas" (p. 146). Vygotsky (1978) refers to the paradoxical nature of play whereby the freedom to enact one's desires in play is tempered by the need to abide by the rules of the play that participants establish.

A comparison can be made between play and storytelling. Livo and Rietz (1986, 5–6) see storytelling as "an act . . . a game we play with events and reality." In storytelling, the storyteller and audience display a strong desire to engage in the storytelling experience and, by doing so, must adhere to the tacit rules for participation and performance. The story opening, "Once upon a time," signals to the audience that the game is about to begin.

While work and play are often seen to be contradictory—work is serious and play is frivolous or childish—Huizinga (in Isenberg & Jalongo 1997) points to the irrelevance of this kind of dualistic opposition: "The play concept itself is of a higher order than is seriousness. For seriousness seeks to exclude play, whereas play can very well include seriousness" (p. 128). Teachers, too, often have competing views of play. For instance, the term *play* can be used generically to refer to child-initiated, as opposed to teacher-directed, activities (again, play versus work), or to activities that are site specific (such as indoor play and outdoor play), or to activities that involve story and storytelling (dramatic play). Play is also considered in relation to children's developmental stages (solitary, parallel, and cooperative play).

At one level, the combination of play and storytelling characterizes activities that form the basis of storytelling workshops. At another level, these activities are derived from a theoretical context and professional framework that encompass principles and assumptions about teaching, learning, and the nature of the learner.

Underlying principles and assumptions

Like good teaching, good storytelling is grounded in principles of active participation, critical reflection, flexibility, and cultural diversity. These principles and their assumptions about the nature of teaching, learning, and the learner undergird both the content and the approach in interesting, exciting storytelling courses.

Active participation

Active participation is the hallmark of a good storytelling course, because simply reading books on storytelling does not provide teachers with the firsthand experience they need in order to know the effects of storytelling on both teller and listener. Storytelling activities are meant to provoke enjoyment, to demonstrate the importance of pleasure in both teaching and learning, and to have application across the curriculum.

Storytelling has always been used to entertain, but it has also been used to teach. Why, then, is storytelling, which is so pervasive in all cultures, so underutilized as a teaching and learning tool?

The most powerful argument to date for using storytelling in teaching is offered by Bruner (1986), who maintains that there are two ways of knowing—narrative and scientific—and both are essential ways of ordering experience. Western education systems may appear to favor abstract thinking, an essential element in scientific thinking, as a higher form of knowing. Nevertheless, narrative plays a key role in the daily social life of classrooms in defining, establishing, and maintaining institutional procedures, rules, and relationships. Narrative also plays an important role in the daily intellectual life of the classroom, in that it is an essential means for conceptualizing, explaining, and understanding the world.

Teaching and learning, teacher and student, are inseparable couplets. To speak of one and not the other is to deny the impact of one upon the other. Each is dependent on the other; otherwise, there is no point to either. Furthermore, both teachers and students are storytellers. That students are storytellers is often neglected in many teacher's guides, which focus on the teacher alone as the traditional storyteller in the classroom. A growing number of professional texts, however, acknowledge the benefits of children as storytellers (e.g., Mallan 1992; Fox 1993; Zipes 1995). Hence, it behooves us to develop ways of encouraging children's storytelling.

Critical reflection

In research on teaching practices and teachers' knowledge, a number of investigators have used the *journal method,* in which teachers record their reflections and stories (Butt, Raymond & Yamagishi 1988; Connelly & Clandinin 1990; Hirsch 1993; Britzman 1995). Many university courses encourage students to keep journals of their experiences, thoughts, questions, and concerns throughout the semester. Journal writing offers a valuable means for students to consider the whys and hows of the learning experiences they engage in during the course of their study and the impact of those experiences on their professional and personal development. The critically reflective thoughts students write in their journals are intended to encourage them to articulate, contextualize, and reexamine their learning (McLean 1993; Kalekin-Fishman 1998).

To elicit student feedback on courses, one can use a range of evaluation techniques. One such technique is the *graffiti board,* a white board in the classroom set aside for students to write comments before or after each class. These comments can take the form of reflections on the course content or on the instructor's approach, questions, frustrations, concerns, good teaching tips, sources for stories, or commentaries on interesting research articles. The graffiti board yields instant feedback and gives students the opportunity to express their immediate questions and reactions. Selections of students' comments can subsequently be reprinted for the benefit of all students and read by the whole class.

Flexibility

By seeing that ideas can be challenged and changed and that knowledge is not something fixed and unchanging, preservice storytelling students learn to view flexibility as a desirable trait to model for their own students. Increasingly, early childhood teachers need to adopt a flexible and responsive teaching approach that takes into account the multiple dynamic social and cultural contexts that influence children's learning, experiences, behaviors, and attitudes. It is important for teachers to accommodate individual and group needs and interests by changing the nature, timing, and location of activities and the groupings of children.

Flexibility of time and place to pursue topics of interest is often difficult to realize in a university environment. Courses are offered over a 14-week semester, and class times are strictly regulated and scheduled. Despite these constraints, flexibility can be woven into the fabric of a course in a number of ways: by providing a range of assignment topics within assessment, by designing open-ended activities that require various groupings of students, and by organizing the physical space of university classrooms so that it is responsive to the demands of the activities at hand. By using flexibility within the parameters of the rules and regulations of both the course and the institution, the instructor can show students that, while there are always constraints operating within any organization, avenues offering different ways of doing things and different perspectives can be explored.

Cultural diversity

As Alloway (1995) has noted, the democratic teaching style adopted by many early childhood educators does not ensure that issues of gender equity and social justice will not arise. Although storytelling has a positive and empowering effect on students, one should be careful not to romanticize it and make universal claims that fail to acknowledge individual differences within classrooms both in early childhood and in university settings.

Storytelling can undoubtedly develop confidence, build self-esteem, foster a sense of community, and enhance oral language skills; however, within the classroom world of never-ending stories, amid the hubbub of voices, silences often go unnoticed. This is true for both children and university students, and it highlights the need for teachers at all levels to be alert to the diverse needs and personalities of the individuals in their classrooms. The silences serve to raise the questions, Whose stories are told? Whose stories are heard? and What meanings are conveyed through these stories? By pausing to consider these questions, teachers create a climate in which the cultural diversity that characterizes their classrooms is acknowledged, celebrated, and respected.

In planning to meet the diverse needs of young children, the early childhood educator must look to all aspects of the educational experience. This examination entails the teacher acknowledging the social and cultural aspects—ethnicity, socioeconomic status, gender, and disability—that circumscribe a child's existence. To this end, certain pedagogical strategies need to be employed, including culturally sensitive activities that promote cooperative learning, a varied range of assessment techniques, and teaching practices that do not limit or constrict student performance to narrow conceptions of gender.

Putting theory into practice

Many of the students who take a course in storytelling become anxious at the prospect of having to tell stories in front of their peers and a university professor. Of course, as instructors, we can assure them that everyone is a storyteller and that not a day goes by when each of us hasn't told someone a story of some kind. However, I find the best way to ease their anxieties is to plunge right into storytelling, beginning with a story about myself. The purpose is to bring home to students that teachers, too, have both strengths and weaknesses—that, like them, teachers experience uncertainty, nervousness, and shyness.

An effective catalyst I have used for eliciting stories from my students is a picture storyboard, which can be made by folding a sheet of paper into four equal parts. In each section, the student creates a simple drawing depicting an experience. For example, the drawings could represent four different emotions—happiness, sadness, embarrassment, and fear. When their storyboards are complete, students listen to and tell their stories in pairs.

In an adaptation of this strategy, the teacher gives each student a small card on which to make a drawing. The cards are then collected, and students are invited to sit in a circle on the floor, with the cards spread out in the center of the circle. Each student selects a drawing that intrigues him or her, and the person who made the drawing tells the other about it. One adaptation for young children is for the teacher to draw pictures on a storyboard.

By using simple, nonthreatening activities such these, the students can come to appreciate the importance of narrative as a way of knowing about themselves and their worlds. Narrative knowledge is not an inferior form of knowledge, and by telling and listening to stories told by both teachers and peers, we can develop a greater understanding of one another and foster a sense of connected knowing (Helle 1991, 54).

Learning to listen and make connections

Teachers must not lose their capacity to listen to their students. The value of being a "kid watcher" has been extolled for a number of years, and teachers have taken on this role with remarkable diligence and perceptiveness. Detailed journal entries and carefully compiled and completed checklists have become the tools for recording our observations about children as they go about the daily business of being learners.

Ironically, in our efforts to document our observations, we run the risk of failing to listen to the child. This point is noted by Vivian Paley, who comments about her early teaching experience, "I was neither a good listener nor an able storyteller when my name became Teacher" (1990, 15). The situation changed, however, when she realized the importance of storytelling in the classroom: "Once I began to view the children as storytellers and playwrights, the potential of fantasy as a learning tool overwhelmed my conventional expectations for the classroom" (p. 19).

At the university level, listening to lectures is one kind of listening. Another kind is active listening, and it demands something special of the listener. That special element is difficult to define, but it entails a willingness to be open to what is being said and perhaps to what is not being said. Bruchac (1997) provides an insight into the importance of this kind of listening:

> It all begins with listening. There are stories everywhere around us, but many people don't notice those stories because they don't take the time to listen. Or if they hear a story being told that is one they've heard, they stop listening. "I've heard that before," they say. Yet if we listen closely to any story, we may hear new things almost every time it is told. (p. 1)

One activity that encourages active listening is inviting students to draw a picture of their childhood home from a bird's-eye view. The students think of the location of their home and those features of the landscape around it. Home is different for different students; it may be a cattle ranch, a small apartment, a house in the suburbs, an orphanage, a houseboat, or a caravan. Some students may have lived in a number of different homes in different towns, cities, or countries. In recalling their surroundings, the students begin to sketch in vegetable gardens, swings, trees, water holes, cattle fences, parks, neighbors' homes, dog kennels, and so on. When the drawings are finished, the teacher may ask the students to locate a story somewhere on their picture. The pictures are then assembled on the floor to form a patchwork of images, and, one by one, pictures are selected and associated stories told.

The preceding exercise alerts students to the importance of home as a defining aspect of one's early experiences. As Bruner (1994) has noted, "Place is crucial and it shapes and constrains the stories that are told or, indeed, that could be told. Place is not simply a piece of geography" (p. 31).

Children encounter different homes and families in the storybooks they read. For many children, these stories bear little resemblance to their own lives. While such fanciful tales have their place in helping children see the "bigger picture," there is also space for their own tale to be told and shared. By encouraging children to talk about their home and neighborhood experiences, we offer them the opportunity to cross the divide that often separates home and school.

Abdullah, Kamberelis, and McGinley (1992) stress the importance of teachers making space in their classrooms for stories by African American children that celebrate their home and community experiences. Such a space, these writers argue, provides ways for children to affirm their historical and cultural identities within the discourse of the classroom. Children of other ethnic or racial minorities undoubtedly benefit as well from this recognition.

Enhancing cultural awareness and understanding

Crosscultural perspectives on storytelling are the main focus of one course I teach. Preservice teachers taking the course are required to read traditional literature from different cultures and tell three stories from different cultural sources to their peers. For reference, I give the students an extensive bibliography of traditional tales and video- and audiotapes of storytellers from different ethnic and racial backgrounds. I also invite local storytellers to tell some tales to the class and to discuss aspects of storytelling from a professional perspective.

Written assignments and other class activities can focus on the cultural aspects of stories and other parts of the curriculum. One of the most enjoyable ways to come to an appreciation of other cultures is through their songs and games. Nearly every song or children's game has a story to tell. The story may be at the surface level of the words and actions (such as the nursery rhyme "Pat-a-Cake") or at a deeper level that conveys historical significance (such as "The Grand Old Duke of York"). As Livo and Rietz (1986) comment,

> The games today are a valuable cultural and human heritage. Like stories, they serve to organize information and to help people understand themselves individually and in the larger frames of reference of community and culture. (p. 302)

These activities can open students' minds to the wealth of stories that exist beyond the more dominant tales shared in schools and help them cross social and cultural boundaries by listening to and telling stories that may strike a responsive chord in all of them.

Cazden (1994) states, "Differences of cultural background and differences in age between teacher and child will affect how the raw tape of experience is edited and transformed" (p. 77). For many children, sharing time (the time the "morning news" gets told) is the official time to relate their experiences, and teachers need to heed Cazden's warning not to edit or transform the children's stories by shaping them to fit their own preferred agenda.

Children come from different cultural and socioeconomic backgrounds, and by the time they enter kindergarten, they have imbibed a varied mix of stories and experiences as both tellers and listeners. For them, storytelling in all its guises has become a central means of organizing their experiences and understanding themselves, their families, and others they encounter in their day-to-day worlds. When we disregard or devalue children's stories as mundane tales (Brodkey 1992), we deny children the sources from which their identities are formed. As Brodkey has explained, this devaluing occurs when teachers engage in the "discursive practice of dismissing difference" (p. 304). (Note, however, that this practice is not confined to teachers, as children themselves are often intolerant of other children's stories, opinions, and interests.)

Conclusion

This chapter began by stating a strong belief about the importance of play and narrative in the lives of both children and adults. When storytelling is offered in university courses and professional development programs, students and teachers can begin to build on their existing knowledge of the power of story for engaging children's minds and emotions. Through such courses, teachers can not only gain confidence in their own abilities to tell stories but also see the benefits of storytelling as a teaching strategy and a means for exploring cultural diversity. By expanding our repertoire of stories to include a wide range of stories—contemporary, traditional, personal, and community—we provide children with opportunities to share and hear stories of difference and diversity. In drawing on such a rich and varied pool of tales, teachers and children will come to a greater understanding of themselves and others.

References

Abdullah, S., G. Kamberelis, & N. McGinley. 1992. Literacy, identity, and resistance within the African-American slave community and some reflections for new forms of literacy. In *Literacy research, theory and practice: Views from many perspectives*, eds. C.K. Kinzor & D.J. Leu, 370–91. Chicago: National Reading Center.

Alloway, N. 1995. *Foundation stones: The construction of gender in early childhood.* Carlton, Victoria, Australia: Curriculum Corporation.

Britton, J. 1992. The anatomy of human experience: The role of inner speech. In *New readings: Contributions to an understanding of literacy*, eds. K. Kimberley, M. Meek, & J. Miller, 146–56. London: Black.

Britzman, D. 1995. "The question of belief": Writing poststructural ethnography. *Qualitative Studies in Education* 8 (3): 229–38.

Brodkey, L. 1992. Articulating poststructural theory in research on literacy. In *Multi-disciplinary perspectives on literacy research*, eds. R. Beach, J. Green, M. Kamil, & T. Shanahan, 293–318. Urbana, IL: National Conference on Research in English and the National Council of Teachers of English.

Bruchac, J. 1997. *Tell me a tale: A book about storytelling.* San Diego: Harcourt Brace.

Bruner, J. 1986. *Actual minds, possible worlds.* Cambridge, MA: Harvard University Press.

Bruner, J. 1994. Life as narrative. In *The need for story: Cultural diversity in classroom and community*, eds. A. Dyson & C. Genishi, 28–37. Urbana, IL: National Council for Teachers of English.

Butt, R., D. Raymond, & L. Yamagishi. 1988. Autobiographical praxis: Studying the formation of teachers' knowledge. *Journal of Curriculum Theorizing* 7 (4): 88–164.

Cazden, C. 1994. What is sharing time for? In *The need for story: Cultural diversity in classroom and community*, eds. A. Dyson & C. Genishi, 72–79. Urbana, IL: National Council for Teachers of English.

Connelly, F.M., & D.J. Clandinin. 1990. Stories of experience and narrative inquiry. *Educational Researcher* 19 (5): 2–14.

Fox, C. 1993. *At the very edge of the forest: The influence of literature on storytelling by children.* London: Cassell.

Helle, A.P. 1991. Reading women's autobiographies: A map of reconstructed knowing. In *Stories lives tell: Narrative and dialogue in education*, eds. C. Witherell & N. Noddings, 48–66. New York: Teachers College Press.

Hirsch, G. 1993. Biography and teacher identity: A typological analysis of life-history data. *Qualitative Studies in Education* 6 (1): 67–83.

Isenberg, J.P., & M.R. Jalongo, eds. 1997. *Creative expression and play in early childhood.* Worthington, OH: Merrill.

Kalekin-Fishman, D. 1998. Teaching EFL: Some concerns. *Educational Practice and Theory* 20 (2): 77–88.

Livo, N., & S. Rietz. 1986. *Storytelling process and practice.* Littleton, CO: Libraries Unlimited.

Mallan, K. 1992. *Children as storytellers.* Portsmouth, NH: Heinemann.

McLean, S.V. 1993. Learning from teachers' stories. *Childhood Education* 69 (5): 265–68.

Paley, V.G. 1990. *The boy who would be a helicopter: The uses of storytelling in the classroom.* Cambridge, MA: Harvard University Press.

Vygotsky, L. 1978. *Mind in society: The development of higher psychological processes.* Cambridge, MA: MIT Press.

Zipes, J. 1995. *Creative storytelling.* New York: Routledge.

Martha Taunton and Cynthia Colbert

7

Art in the Early Childhood Classroom: Authentic Experiences and Extended Dialogues

A visit to an early childhood classroom clearly reveals the integral role of visual arts in the education of young children. Along with the absorbing activities and intense verbal conversations of children and teachers, the inspired artworks created by children are both a part of the process and a testament to the learning accomplished in the setting.

These works of art, spontaneous and reflective, intricate and bold, complex and direct, reveal the hearts and minds of children. We see the amazing work of which young children are capable when teachers make visual arts education a powerful, integral part of the early childhood curriculum. From studies of classrooms, we know the primacy of the visual arts in the development of young children's expression and communication, their presence in children's daily lives, and their critical use by educators.

Valuing the visual arts

Most recently, our exposure to the ideas and physical evidence of teaching from the preschools of Reggio Emilia, Italy, (Thompson 1995; Edwards, Gandini, & Forman 1998; Topal & Gandini 1999) has emphasized the value of the visual arts for the young child and in the early childhood classroom, as have the earlier theories of Vygotsky (1962, 1978) and the study of constructivism. In many magnet schools and in programs modeled after Reggio schools, the visual arts are at the center of children's learning. These programs demonstrate how children use drawing, painting, collage, construction, or modeling to learn about their world. Children create physical representations of people, places, and objects to better understand them.

For young children, art making is a way of gaining control over a task, a way of seeing a problem and making sense of it and its parts, a way of understanding. Colbert describes the process:

> Children are intrinsically motivated to create art and become fully engaged in the artistic process. Children also demonstrate a strong sense of purpose when they make art. . . . [they] are consciously working to express their ideas through their symbols and images. Through their art, children reveal their individual thoughts, feelings and moods and through symbols they describe their very existence with sophistication and simplicity, often leaving adults in awe of their powerful and authentic voice. (1997, 201)

Burton (1994, 2000) contributes to this argument for the arts and describes the value of the arts in the development and education of children.

> If in the fashioning of visual images, children transform human experience into artistic content, and if this also calls on how they make sense of and learn from the artistry of others, then this is a critical argument for supporting the importance of artistry to human growth and development. . . . But in order for human experience to become artistic content it must first be shaped in a medium and imbued with artistic presence. (1994, 483)

To have a significant role in early childhood education, art experiences must be authentic in approach and content and include opportunities for children's reflection through extended classroom dialogues. Authentic art experiences in the classroom are organized through a teacher's knowledge of patterns of artistic and aesthetic development, consideration of the intentions of children as they make art, and recognition of significant content in the subject of art and art's relationship to other disciplines.

Extended dialogues include intimate conversations between teachers and children as children work, reflective discussions about children's completed artworks, and discussions about art in everyday life, by their peers and professional artists, and in other cultures. Additionally, extended dialogues refer to those continuing conversations between teachers and children that powerfully connect one learning experience with another.

This vision of the visual arts does not separate them from the larger classroom experience but rather seeks to embed art experiences in the process of learning and to give artistic form to expressions of learning.

Artistic and aesthetic development

Children's artistic and aesthetic development has a rich, documented research history. As a result we know a great deal about children's early artistic and aesthetic development, and this knowledge informs our practice with young children. Children's artistic developmental sequence does not fall neatly into Piagetian stages but does parallel most theories of child development. Stages in artistic development do not have discrete beginnings and endings in the developmental sequence, but rather children exhibit a tendency to move back and forth between stages as they learn and grow.

Children's intentions in the drawing process differ from those of adult artists. In young children's drawing development, there are individual and gender differences in developmental patterns. Girls, on the average, are ahead of boys by up to six months in producing a complete figure with double lines for both arms and legs.

Configurations such as humans without trunks, or tadpole figures, are completely normal in a child's acquisition of drawing abilities (Figure 1). The kinesthetic pleasure young children enjoy in their earliest mark making provides a foundation for their communication with beginning symbols, which in time enables children to develop complete and complex narratives (Figure 2) (Taunton & Colbert 1984; Cox 1993, 1997; Kindler 1997; Hanes & Weisman 2000).

Figure 1. *Three drawings by a 3-year-old girl, completed in succession: figure without the trunk, figure with skirt, figure with trunk*

Research on children's aesthetic development reveals patterns of development in how children perceive and understand their visual world and the visual arts, which can guide early childhood classroom teachers (Taunton & Colbert 1984). Young children perceive subtle aspects of artworks, although they may be unable to verbalize these distinctions. They can state art preferences and support their preferences, but these preferences may fluctuate from day to day.

Young children recognize that different people have different points of view and different opinions about the same object. Judgmental criteria shift from obvious favorites of color and subject matter during the preschool and early elementary years to more complex judgments based on an appreciation of realism, conceptions of appropriate subject matter, and expressive significance. Older children acknowledge artists' intentions and the social nature of artworks in their aesthetic understanding and judgment (Parsons 1987; Hobbs & Rush 1997).

Knowing how children develop their ideas in drawings and sculpture and how they respond to their artwork and the work of others is important for those who teach. Art instruction that focuses on representation, detail, or accuracy at a stage when children are prerepresentational or beginning to form symbols is inappropriate and disregards the child's natural sequence of development. With an understanding of patterns in

Figure 2. *Spaceship launch by a boy, age 4*

children's artistic development, teachers can introduce problems having potentially multiple and divergent solutions, representing all developmental levels in the classroom, and presenting interesting and appropriate challenges.

Teachers can ensure that children have opportunities to discuss with others what they see when they look at art, state their own preferences and evaluations, and explore verbally the basis for their own and others' views. Teachers also can model the use of rich and varied descriptive and metaphoric language in responding to art as well as carefully structure classroom inquiry about artworks (Taunton & Colbert 1984).

Classroom research and art education with young children

The teacher is pivotal in organizing classroom dialogue, learning materials and objects, the classroom environment, and explicit curriculum expectations into experiences that encourage and develop children's learning. Research of early childhood art experiences provides insight into the relationship between art learning and social and contextual factors and how the actions of teachers steer the art learning of young children in particular directions (Colbert & Taunton in press).

Teachers shape the context for art

Teachers make influential decisions about the structure of an art task, the amount of time allowed for art, the art materials used, and the accessibility of materials. Teachers decide whether to use models or teacher-made examples to illustrate solutions. They also select artists' and children's artworks for display in the classroom.

Classroom studies show that these decisions set up explicit and implicit criteria for children's artwork and may convey conceptions about sub-ject matter and materials appropriate for art as well as about the nature of art (Colbert & Taunton in press). Often these conceptions reflect an adult's preference for realism, neatness, and acceptable ways to use materials and imply that art is an activity resulting in a product, not a process and a personal expression of learning.

Teachers influence classroom discourse

These same teacher decisions influence the focus, and thus the content, of classroom discourse. For example, if certain materials needed for an art activity are physically difficult for young children to use, the discussions during work time may be consumed by conversations on how to do the physical part of the task rather than about ideas children want to express, descriptive qualities of materials and their potential for expression, or the use of aesthetic elements to communicate ideas. Adult comments that ask children to name their artwork or describe their work also may elicit children's responses to adult expectations of realism rather than expressions about their ideas or artwork.

Well-timed, well-considered dialogues initiated by teachers as children work are opportunities for increased critical reflection and personal extensions of learning. Such discussions help children develop artistic and aesthetic content as well as descriptive and elaborate language, critical thinking, planning skills, and problem-solving strategies.

Teachers must consider children's developmental levels and intentions for these dialogues to have meaning. Teachers can plan dialogues in which they guide children's descriptive language and ask children to reflect upon their actions, such as their use of line, color, or certain imagery, to convey their intended meaning (Rosario & Collazo 1981; Sharp 1981; Smith 1983; Taunton 1983, 1986; Alexander 1984; Swann 1987; Colbert & Taunton in press).

Teachers design the environment

Teachers also make decisions about the classroom environment that affect art learning. Studies show that teachers plan areas for discussions, walls for displays, centers for activities, and areas for supplies (Colbert & Taunton in press). In the organization of these classroom areas by teachers and their use by children, the spaces and artifacts take on meaning and influence learning. Through their classroom routines children become aware of appropriate activities for these areas, including discussing and critiquing art, reading about art, and doing art work. Interesting objects serve as catalysts for personal explorations and informal discussions by children.

The rich environment of an early childhood classroom in which children are studying Japan illustrates how teachers use the environment to teach. In the classroom are elegant kimonos for display and play, Japanese dolls in traditional costume, Japanese bonsai plants, photographs of Japanese gardens, reproductions of Japanese art, Japanese kites and calendars, and books about Japan. Children's artworks are displayed and include origami, small paper and plasticene models of Japanese lunch boxes or *okibanas*, fish prints, and small Japanese gardens.

Children's spontaneous discussions each day usually focus on the surrounding objects that make concrete the everyday culture of the Japanese people. These interesting objects extend the learning in a direction that was begun by the teacher but determined by the children (Pariser 1981; Taunton 1986).

Classroom practice: Art education within early childhood education

The visual arts understandably have a significant presence in many early childhood classrooms. The approach, goals, and content of visual arts education and early childhood education clearly mesh.

Art education encourages children to link their knowledge and experiences with communication in concrete and meaningful ways. Art education also invites children to learn through their senses and to make connections by comparing, ordering, measuring, and making associations. Teachers of art remain open to children's interpretations of their experiences and encourage children to create works that reflect who they are and their personalities, interests, and skills and involve them in learning through exploration and investigation.

Visual arts bring disciplines together

Early childhood teachers have discovered the visual arts' powerful way of bringing an interdisciplinary unit together. Through appropriate uses of the visual arts, language arts, literature, social studies, mathematics, science, movement, and music come to life (Bredekamp & Copple 1997; Colbert 1997; Colbert & Brooks 2000).

Many educators outside the field of art education support the role of art making, specifically drawing, in the development of children's language and writing skills. Gallas (1994) writes about her class of elementary school children and her recognition that some children are natural scientists, authors, mathematicians, and artists in their approaches to learning. Hubbard and Ernst (1996) show how writing, art, and reading can be successfully combined in different content areas. In her earlier work, Hubbard (1989) uses drawing and writing almost interchangeably in her classroom. Her descriptions of the children's work illustrate not just the coupling of drawing and literacy but the interrelationship between the two.

Although often included as an area of study in interdisciplinary formats, in the early childhood classroom the visual arts have a unique place. Teaching with the visual arts enables young children to construct their learning and extend, reflect, and make it tangible in artistic forms and through classroom dialogues.

Integrating art enhances learning and expression

Several drawings by young children, with descriptions of the classroom experiences in which the drawings were made, illustrate that art education embedded in an early childhood program creates a supportive, challenging learning process and a form for expressions of learning.

The map of a kindergarten child's bedroom (Figure 3) was done in a teacher's introductory art unit, with "Night" as the broad theme. The unit included a study of phases of the moon, constellations, space, nocturnal animals, and children's literature related to night. Children talked about how they spent their nights and drew maps of their

Figure 3. *Map of a 5-year-old girl's bedroom, with teacher notations*

rooms as one of several art experiences related to this unit. The maps reflected children's different developmental levels, but all were personal, individual, and revealing. The mapmaking required children to consider how to represent a three-dimensional space, which they knew well, in two dimensions with line and color.

A collection of preschool drawings of animals by children ages 3 to 5 (Figure 4) is a second example. Following a class discussion of pets, children made small line drawings (approximately three inches square) of pets they had or pets they would like to have. The children sorted the two sets of drawings into categories, such as fish, cats, and dogs, and counted the drawings in each category. The teacher helped assemble the two sets of drawings to form two bar graphs: "pets we have" and "pets we would like to have."

To complete their drawings, children had to remember or imagine pets, clarify distinctions between animals such as how a cat is different from a dog, and develop graphic forms and use media to show these distinctions. The process of assembling the drawings into bar graphs required children to sort, count, estimate, compare, and organize information.

Figure 4. *Animal drawings by preschoolers, ages 3 to 5*

Developing Meaningful Learning Opportunites

Figure 5. *Observation drawings of plants by a kindergartner and a first-grader, ages 6 and 7*

Children completed a third set of drawings (Figure 5) as part of a unit in which the organizing theme was a broad study of art. Paired as partners, kindergarten and first-grade children selected a plant from an assortment of two- to three-inch potted plants in their classroom. Each set of partners drew, painted, collaged, or modeled their plants. In this experience the children observed and recorded their observations, looked again, and looked with others. They noted differences in plant structures. They discussed the different ways that artists work as styles of art. They discovered ways that many artists and scientists record and develop ideas. The children also learned about style and point-of-view as they saw how one another represented the same object in different ways.

The teachers in these classrooms created the kind of authentic art experiences that occur in the many early childhood classrooms of exceptional teachers. The experiences are characterized by the teachers' focus on appropriate curriculum themes and guided by children's interests and developmental perspectives.

The experiences also embody teaching strategies that reveal the early childhood teachers' knowledge of artistic and cognitive development and of practices that link artistic process and content to that of other disciplines. The experiences use art materials appropriate for the children and the task; they demonstrate different ways teachers organize classrooms and children in centers, stations, small and large groups, pairs and as individuals to facilitate learning.

These experiences involve children looking at and discussing related artwork of artists and illustrators in conjunction with their own efforts. The teachers orchestrating these experiences support, challenge, and respond to children through organization and dialogue and encourage children to learn through their fashioning of personal visions.

Professional development in visual arts for young children

If these are the kinds of things we want teachers to do, then what professional development do we need to provide? To make a wide range of informed decisions on classroom practice in the visual arts, early childhood professionals need to set some goals that include the following:

• To gain an understanding of children's artistic and aesthetic development and how this relates to other areas of learning and development—emotional, intellectual, motor, perceptual, social, and creative

• To understand what visual arts education is and what it is not

• To become familiar with methods, materials, practices, and procedures of teaching art in early childhood settings

• To gain knowledge of age-appropriate and developmentally appropriate teaching of basic art concepts and methods as well as use of art images and materials

• To learn how to look at and talk about art so as to engage in meaningful conversations with children about their artworks

• To become acquainted with philosophies of aesthetics and art criticism and the history of art to enable your discussion of artists' works with children and the encouragement of children to become discerning viewers of images

• To gain a knowledge of the elements of art and principles of design and experiences in their practice

• To develop skill in making interdisciplinary connections between the visual arts and other areas of the early childhood curriculum

To acquire the prerequisite knowledge and skills to work effectively with the visual arts, teachers-in-training need various kinds of experiences. They need to work with a wide range of art materials and processes, guided by visual arts educators who model the kinds of interactions that teachers themselves will later have with children. Also important are opportunities to observe young children engaged in art, especially in early childhood programs that are exemplary in integrating the visual arts. Of course, seeing knowledgeable, skilled teachers in action is an essential aspect

of professional development in visual arts, as in any subject area.

Students and inservice participants also need many opportunities to engage with young children in visual arts experiences. As they do this, students gain confidence in the area of visual arts—unfamiliar and intimidating to many of them—as well as skill in interacting with children as they explore, create, and discuss their artworks and the artworks of others.

We recommend that early childhood professionals take at least one course in visual arts education and that an integrated arts approach be part of their curriculum. To design options for both preservice and inservice teachers, teacher educators and departments of education need to collaborate closely with arts faculty. Community arts organizations, regional institutes, and other groups outside the college or university also can be good resources for early childhood educators. In different communities, professional development in the visual arts will take distinct shapes and configurations suited to the particular needs and resources of the community.

Conclusion

Young children observe, inquire about, and imagine the world around them. Creating art is one way children gain understanding, and translating their perceptions into visual forms is for young children a natural way of making meaning. Early childhood classroom teachers have the opportunity and challenge of working with children at a stage when they are rapidly developing language and cognitive skills. They see children's early development of symbols and the beginning of narratives. They hear the profound questions that young children ask.

Early childhood educators can become facilitators of children's inquiry when they respect the processes and ideas of children engaged in artistic explorations with materials to create visual forms. Knowing what materials to offer for different kinds of expression, how to nurture a child's personal style and to encourage development, and how to commend children's artistic efforts are important skills for teachers.

Teachers who skillfully engage in meaningful dialogues with children about their work are nurturing young children's development of authentic voices. When teachers help children to fully engage in an activity that allows them to express themselves in symbols, forms, and images, they enable them to learn and better understand themselves and their world.

Education in the visual arts should enable early childhood professionals to make good instructional decisions, know what child art is and is not, and seamlessly use the visual arts to explore and make instruction personally meaningful for children. The teacher's role is to facilitate children's natural ways of expression while enhancing their understandings of what they see and create about the world in a painting, drawing, modeling, or construction. By providing a nurturing and encouraging atmosphere, appropriate materials, and substantive dialogue with each child, the early childhood educator enhances children's artistic development.

References

Alexander, R.R. 1984. First-graders' classroom conversations about art making: Social life, fantasy and play, verisimilitude, and media/procedures. Paper presented at the annual meeting of the American Educational Research Association Meeting, April 4–8, New Orleans.

Bredekamp, S., & C. Copple, eds. 1997. *Developmentally appropriate practice in early childhood programs.* Rev. ed. Washington, DC: NAEYC.

Burton, J.M. 1994. The arts in school reform. *Teachers College Record* 95 (4): 477–93.

Burton, J.M. 2000. The configuration of meaning: Learner-centered art education revisited. *Studies in Art Education* 41 (4): 330–45.

Colbert, C. 1997. Visual arts in the developmentally appropriate integrated curriculum In *Integrated curriculum and developmentally appropriate practice,* eds. C. Hart, D.C. Burts, & R. Charlesworth, 201–23. Albany: State University of New York Press.

Colbert, C., & R. Brooks. 2000. *Connections in art. The interdisciplinary art-based curriculum for grades 1–5.* Worcester, MA: Davis.

Colbert, C., & M. Taunton. In press. Classroom research in the visual arts. In *American Educational Research Association handbook on classroom research,* ed. V. Richardson. New York: Macmillan.

Cox, M. 1993. *Children's drawings of the human figure.* Hove, UK: Lawrence Erlbaum.

Cox, M. 1997. *Drawings of people by the under-5s.* London, UK: Falmer.

Edwards, C., L. Gandini, & G. Forman, eds. 1998. *The hundred languages of children: The Reggio Emilia approach—Advanced reflections.* 2d ed. Greenwich, CT: Ablex.

Gallas, K . 1994. *The languages of learning: How children talk, write, chance, draw, and sing their understanding of the world.* New York: Teachers College Press.

Hanes, J.M., & E. Weisman. 2000. Observing a child use drawing to find meaning. *Art Education* 53 (1): 6–11.

Hobbs, J. A., & J.C. Rush. 1997. *Teaching children's art.* Upper Saddle River, NJ: Prentice Hall.

Hubbard, R.S. 1989. *Authors of pictures, draughtsmen of words.* Portsmouth, NH: Heinemann.

Hubbard, R.S., & K. Ernst. 1996. *New entries: Learning by writing and drawing.* Portsmouth, NH: Heinemann.

Kindler, A.M., ed. 1997. *Child development in art.* Reston, VA: National Art Education Association.

Pariser, D. 1981. Linear lessons in a centrifugal environment: An ethnographic sketch of an art teaching experience. *Review of Research in Visual Arts Education* 9: 81–90.

Parsons, M.J. 1987. *How we understand art.* Cambridge, UK: Cambridge University.

Rosario, J., & E. Collazo. 1981. Aesthetic codes in context: An exploration in two preschool classrooms. *Journal of Aesthetic Education* 15 (1): 71–82.

Sharp, P. 1981. The development of aesthetic response in early education. Ph.D. diss., Stanford University.

Smith, N.R. 1983. *Experience and art: Teaching children to paint*. New York: Teachers College Press.

Swann, A. 1987. Child/adult interaction during art activities in a preschool setting: An achievement seeking response. In *Conference proceedings, AERA/arts and learning research, vol. 4*, ed. C. Colbert, 73–79. Columbia: University of South Carolina.

Taunton, M. 1983. Ways to talk and what to say: A study of art conversations among young children and adults in pre-school settings. In *AERA/arts and learning SIG proceedings, vol. 1*, ed. M. Taunton, 1–14. Iowa City: University of Iowa.

Taunton, M. 1986. The conveyance of aesthetic values during art activities in grades one through three. *Journal of Multicultural Research in Art Education* 2: 10–16.

Taunton, M., & C. Colbert. 1984. Artistic and aesthetic development: Considerations for early childhood educators. *Childhood Education* 61 (1): 55–63.

Thompson, C.M., ed. 1995. *The visual arts and early childhood learning*. Reston, VA: National Art Education Association.

Topal, C.W., & L. Gandini. 1999. *Beautiful stuff.* Worcester, MA: Davis.

Vygotsky, L. 1962. *Thought and language*. Cambridge, MA: MIT Press.

Vygotsky, L. 1978. *Mind in society: The development of higher psychological processes*. Cambridge, MA: Harvard University Press.

Kym Irving

8

Innovations in Observing Children: Use of New Technologies

O bservation of young children plays a pivotal role in early childhood education, for a number of reasons. Historically, observing children has served as the foundation for curriculum planning and has enabled teachers to center their programs on the specific needs of individual children.

The early years, from birth to age 8, are distinguished by profound changes in all areas of development, with astonishing advances in physical, motor, cognitive, social, and emotional development. Add to these an array of individual variations in developmental pathways and timing, and it is clear why observation of children is one of the core undertakings of early childhood educators. Indeed, for educators working with infants and toddlers, observation is the primary means of discovering children's interests, fears, likes, dislikes, and sources of pleasure and satisfaction. Finally, the appreciation of young children's capacities to learn is achieved largely through observation.

The challenge

The professional observation of children is best undertaken in the context of warm, supportive relationships characterized by adult attentiveness to the children's verbal and non-verbal signals and an understanding of the meaning and importance of the children's behaviors in the contexts in which they are observed. Accordingly, as a teacher educator in early childhood, I am duty bound to help students develop both their attentiveness to children and their understanding of the significance of children's behavior for learning.

Early childhood education students in my courses have traditionally developed their professional rapport with children in two ways: informally, through their contacts with the children of friends and relatives, and more formally, through their practicum experiences in field settings. In recent years, a number of issues have arisen to challenge the assumption that students can effectively develop the skills of observation and analysis in those settings. These issues can be summarized as follows.

• *Reductions in field experience.* Cuts in funding and the competing demands of various course content areas have led to reductions in the time devoted to field experiences in many early childhood teacher preparation programs. These reductions limit students' time for developing skills during the practicum. Often, beginning students feel overwhelmed by the variety of tasks facing them. Students express concern about the amount of time they have to (a) immerse themselves in the tasks associated with observation, (b) reflect on what they observe, and (c) discuss their observations and interpretations with others. The challenge is finding more effective and innovative ways to provide students with opportunities for learning about observing children prior to their practica.

• *Making connections.* When students are pressured for time, they tend to make observations that accurately record the behaviors of children but lack a deeper appreciation of the significance of those behaviors. Failure to appreciate the significance of children's behaviors seems to relate to the difficulty students experience in connecting the theoretical and empirical descriptions of children's development with what the students observe. Here, the challenge is to provide students with clear examples of the child behaviors described in their texts and readings.

• *Accuracy and significance.* Finally, the observational records that students make during the practicum and in other settings often are done independently of the university teaching staff. That is, university teachers frequently are not present while the students are recording their observations and, therefore, may be unsure as to whether the students have recorded those observations accurately and reliably. Indeed, students may miss many child behaviors that hold significance for subsequent interpretation and planning. In this regard, the challenge is to get staff involved at the time the students are observing and recording, in order to afford extra insights that might better scaffold students' early learning about children in these contexts.

A solution: Bringing the outside in

Clearly, one solution to the problem is to provide students with experiences that

• give them sufficient time for recording, interpreting, reflecting upon, and discussing their observations of children;

• enable them to engage in repeated practice and analysis;

• make clear the links between theoretical descriptions and children's real-life behavior; and

• afford a degree of involvement by lecturing staff, such that accuracy is maintained and scaffolding strengthened.

Given these criteria, in our institution we resolved to package real-world examples of children that would maximize student learning about observing children and about child development. Our knowledge of research suggested that a computer-based multimedia approach would best suit our aim and would be an effective and efficient means of bringing the outside (children and their behavior) *into* the learning contexts of college students, studying on or off campus.

Why multimedia?

The decision to use a multimedia approach stemmed from an analysis of emergent trends in the use of multimedia programs in all areas of education (Barker 1993; Aston & Schwarz 1994; Willis et al. 1997; Ivers & Barron 1998). The promotion of multimedia in higher education has arisen from the recognition that universities now cater to an array of sophisticated learners who increasingly expect state-of-the-art teaching and learning approaches in their

Developing Meaningful Learning Opportunities

courses. This expectation is realistic, given the pressure that graduates in education will experience from the community to create similar opportunities for their children

Aside from the argument that beginning teachers should be conversant and current in computers and technology, a range of educational benefits has been attributed to the use of multimedia in computer-based education. Among these benefits are the promotion of student mastery of content and skills, positive perceptions of the amount of learning achieved, increased levels of interest, a greater desire to continue studying the subject, increased sense of control over learning, and improvements in hypothesis-generating and testing skills (Krendl & Lieberman 1988; Alexander & Frampton 1994).

If learning is viewed as an active, constructive process that is influenced not only by the learner's internal characteristics (e.g., knowledge, interest, and self-efficacy) but also by external characteristics of the learning environment, then environments that offer a range of methods and tools are more likely to support a variety of learners. The inclusion of multimedia programs in postsecondary teaching allows a greater choice and flexibility of learning for a broader range of students.

A further reason for adopting a multimedia approach is that its use gives rise to several benefits for teacher education in particular. The use of interactive videotapes is not new to teacher education, with applications covering classroom simulations, classroom management, and decisionmaking (Cruikshank 1986; Goldman & Barron 1990; Berry 1994; Overbaugh 1995). Indeed, evaluations of such applications suggest that the use of videotapes to familiarize students with tasks they will face in the classroom enables students to engage more effectively in real situations. Furthermore, video simulations provide actual data from which students can draw conclusions and build strategies that they may later implement. In that way, simulations allow students to engage in information processing that then guides their own behavior.

A video clip of two young children engaged in a minor dispute over toys, for example, demonstrates the "antecedents, behaviors, consequences" format of an observation technique called *event sampling*. At the same time, the user's attention is drawn to the educator's response to the children. The educator's strategy is one possible course of action, but students' own evaluations of the situation may lead them to any one of a number of decisions concerning strategy. Students who view the educator's strategy as ineffective or at variance with their teaching philosophies are likely to discard it. Others who see the strategy as having value might incorporate it into their own repertoires. Some students may refine the strategy into a more effective approach.

In sum, through the use of simulations, reflection, and discussion, students build strategies that can later be implemented in field settings with children and assessed for efficacy.

Anticipated benefits

As previously mentioned, the benefits to students of a multimedia approach are numerous and varied, but two benefits in particular were deemed to relate to the aims of our multimedia project: the refinement of students' observational and interpretative skills through their ability to repeatedly review children's behavior (Grabe & Tabor 1981; Collyer 1984) and the provision of opportunities for self-paced, autonomous learning or, if preferred, small-group learning, by taking advantage of a multimedia computer environment (Hooper & Hannafin 1991). The latter benefit would make available extended learning opportunities to students living far from the campus.

Finally, we identified some benefits that were tangential to the main aims of the project. These had to do with contributing to the technological literacy of beginning early childhood teachers. Preservice courses play a major role in helping shape the competencies of teachers in this area, and the project was seen as providing opportunities for students to develop their understanding of computer-based learning.

Description of the project

Our institution's multimedia project was made possible through a large injection of funds from the university and a great deal of technical assistance. To date, the project has incorporated the development of two CD-ROMs: "Observing and Analyzing Young Children's Behavior" (Irving & Tennent 1998) and "Exploring Young Children's Development." The main phases of design, development, and evaluation of the CDs have required input and feedback from many staff and students. (See "Model for Tasks Associated with the Multimedia Project" on the opposite page.)

When the first CD-ROM— on child observation techniques (Irving & Tennent 1998)—was developed, it was immediately integrated into early childhood courses at several universities. This CD-ROM illustrates, through detailed graphics and interactive exercises, six techniques for recording child behavior: running records, anecdotal records, time samples, event samples, checklists, and rating scales. It also affords students practice in the use of the six techniques through on-screen video clips of children in a variety of settings. Students are able to pause and review the video sequences as often as they wish, and they have control over the pace at which they work through the learning activities.

The second CD-ROM, which is currently under development, focuses on observing specific areas of children's development in the social, cognitive, language, motor, and play domains. In this CD-ROM, students' difficulties in connecting developmental theory with observations of children are addressed through the repeated use of examples (video, audio, graphics, and text) that highlight concepts, phases, and features of children's development. A range of activities is used to engage and strengthen students' learning.

The CD-ROMs are flexible in that, while some segments follow a linear progression for beginning students, others allow advanced students to explore their own topics. The CD-ROMs incorporate the following features aimed at stimulating user interest:

• video and audio segments to illustrate children's behavior and development

• graphics to illustrate difficult concepts (e.g., the notion of prototypes in the development of categories)

• various interactive features, from click-and-drag exercises to on-screen activities, such as exploring a fantasy room in order to understand the factors that influence awareness of the environment and identifying language functions in a videotaped segment of two children interacting with each other

• on-screen notepads for students to respond to open-ended exercises and to record notes and reflections

• a glossary and a reference list

• multiple-choice and open-ended exercises for self-evaluation, review of material, and tutorial discussion

Evaluation

Testing and evaluation of the first CD-ROM indicated a high level of user interest, with a number of students preferring the computer-based materials to textbooks, lectures, and videos. Feedback from students also reinforced the design and content features of the modules. An important finding was that students perceived the simulations as providing practice opportunities that might not otherwise be available to them during field experiences because of competing demands on their time and attention.

Model for Tasks Associated with the Multimedia Project

Phase	Activity	Purpose	Questions	Approaches
Design	Needs analysis	To provide information for planning and design	• What areas of child observation and behavior present students with the most difficulty? • Is a multimedia program an appropriate way to deal with these difficulties?	• Seek information and expertise • Discuss with university support-services staff having expertise in computer-based learning • Review learners and learning context
	Project team formation	To inform and develop the content and instructional and technical features of the program	• How and in what form will information be conveyed? • What are the technical requirements?	• Form project team comprising content experts, programmers, instructional designers, graphic designers
	Formative evaluation	To inform decisions about the design of the program	• What educational strategy should be used? • Is the user-interface appropriate?	• Review literature on student learning with multimedia • Develop prototype
Develop	Content development	To identify relevant content, learning goals, and instructional aims	• What and how are students learning? • Is the package a valid approach to addressing the stated learning needs?	• Testing by technical and content experts • Testing by students using observation, user-tracking, interviews, and questionnaires
	Formative evaluation	To inform development of the program	• What is the merit of the program?	• Expert and peer review
Integrate	Summative evaluation	To determine the worth of the program in the context of its use	• What changes in understanding and skills have students undergone?	• Pre and post interviews/discussions with students and staff • Analysis of student work
Institutionalize	Impact evaluation	To determine the transfer of changes in understanding and skills to field settings	• Do students apply their new skills and understandings to the field? • What has been the impact on other areas of curriculum, learning, and the organization?	• Wider discussions and interviews with students, practica supervisors, and teachers in field • Interviews and data gathering over time • Expert review
	Maintenance evaluation	To determine the program's ongoing validity and currency	• Is the program continuing to be valid?	

Source: Adapted by permission, from S. Alexander & J. Hedberg, "Evaluating Technology-Based Learning: Which Model?" In *Interactive Multimedia in University Education: Designing for Change in Teaching and Learning,* eds. K. Beattie, C. McNaught, & S. Wills (Amsterdam: Elsevier, 1994).

Students' reactions

To determine whether the general aim of the project was being met by the package, we asked students to comment on their experiences with the CD-ROM. Their responses were favorable to many of the incorporated features. For example, one students offered the following comment on how the package allowed self-paced learning and reviewing:

> I like the setup of the modules—they are easy to use, read, and understand. Reading the description, then studying the sample and doing the exercise with immediate feedback is great—it helps reinforce the observation techniques being "taught."

Students also found the CD-ROM less intimidating than traditional approaches and with no risk of opprobrium if they responded wrongly to a question. In addition, they recognized the advantages of developing their skills before encountering children in early childhood environments. One student stated,

> I think it's a great way to learn about observation techniques. It does seem a better method than disrupting the classroom or day care environment.

Students found the exercises beneficial and enjoyable and commented on features that corresponded with the design aims of the package—for example, that it should provide concise, revisable information and clear, sequential development of skills.

A number of comments pertained to the constraints that the package imposed and served as a reminder that computer-based materials are only one of a number of learning tools that should ultimately give way to learning in situ. One student in particular made this point, stating,

> I still feel that "real" observational settings are important. Hands-on experience can never truly be replaced by something that is computer generated; however, the use of this package allows us to practice observation techniques without the hassles that field experience can sometimes generate. It gives us a chance to polish techniques, so to speak, without disturbing a class situation. Then, when we are in a practical situation, we have the observational skills necessary to utilize our practical experience.

The future

In the short term, we anticipate that students will gain an understanding of observational strategies and child behavior when engaged in the multimedia learning. In the longer term, students are expected to transfer observational, problem-solving, and planning skills they learn from computer-based instruction to the field setting. A successful transfer will be reflected in the quality of the students' field observations, their interpretations of child behavior, and their plans for subsequent education in the field. These improvements in teacher education will further enhance the professional skills of graduates of early childhood education programs so that they can plan children's education more effectively.

Designing and developing multimedia materials is just the first step in the process of creating innovative learning tools for students preparing to become early childhood educators. The materials must also meet the criterion of being high-quality learning tools, a criterion that critics argue is infrequently applied. For that reason, ongoing formative and summative evaluations by all of the learners in the project (staff and students) will serve as the basis for continual refinement and improvement of the project materials.

References

Alexander, M., & D. Frampton. 1994. Technology and thinking: A qualitative study with interactive multimedia products. Paper presented at the Second Interactive Multimedia Symposium, January, in Perth, Australia.

Alexander, S., & J. Hedberg. 1994. Evaluating technology-based learning: Which model? In *Interactive multimedia in university education: Designing for change in teaching and learning,* eds. K. Beattie, C. McNaught, & S. Wills. Amsterdam: Elsevier.

Aston, A., & J. Schwarz. 1994. *Multimedia: Gateway to the next millennium.* Boston: AP Professional.

Barker, B. 1993. Using instructional technologies in the preparation of teachers for the twenty-first century. Paper presented at the National Conference on Creating the Quality School, March, in Oklahoma City, Oklahoma.

Berry, L.H. 1994. Interactive video simulations: Factors related to promoting teacher effectiveness. In *Technology and teacher education annual,* ed. J. Willis. Proceedings of the Annual Conference of the Society for Technology and Teacher Education. ERIC, ED 412921.

Collyer, C. 1984. Using computers in the teaching of psychology: Five things that seem to work. *Teaching of Psychology* 11: 206–09.

Cruikshank, D.R. 1986. Instructional alternatives available for use in professional education. In *Simulation and clinical knowledge in teacher education: Prologue for the future,* ed. E. Doak. Proceedings from a national invitational symposium. Knoxville: University of Tennessee.

Goldman, E., & L. Barron. 1990. Using hypermedia to improve the preparation of elementary teachers. *Journal of Teacher Education* 41: 21–31.

Grabe, M., & L. Tabor. 1981. The use of videotaped material in the instruction and evaluation of developmental psychology students. *Teaching of Psychology* 8: 115–17.

Hooper, S., & M. Hannafin. 1991. The effects of group composition on achievement, interaction, and learning efficiency during computer-based cooperative instruction. *Educational Technology Research and Development* 39 (3): 27–40.

Irving, K., & Tennent, L. 1998. Observing and analysing young children's behaviour (CD-ROM). Sydney, Australia: Prentice Hall.

Ivers, K.S., & A. Barron. 1998. *Multimedia projects in education: Designing, producing, and assessing.* Englewood, CO: Libraries Unlimited.

Krendl, K., & D. Lieberman. 1988. Computers and learning: A review of recent research. *Journal of Educational Computing Research* 4 (4): 367–89.

Overbaugh, R.C. 1995. The efficacy of interactive video for teaching basic classroom management skills to pre-service teachers. *Computers in Human Behavior* 11: 511–27.

Willis, J., J. Price, S. McNeil, B. Robin, & D. Willis. 1997. *Technology and teacher education annual,* vol. 1, 2. Proceedings of the International Conference of the Society for Information Technology and Teacher Education (SITE) in Orlando, Florida.

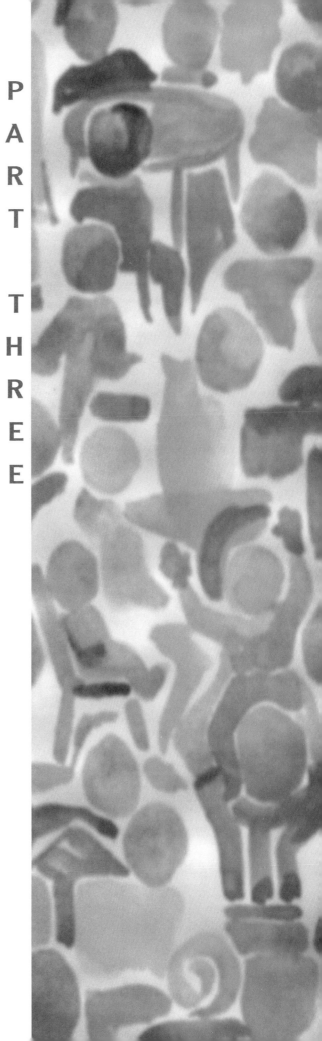

Creating
Communities
for Learning

Susan Grieshaber and Carmel Diezmann

9

The Challenge of Teaching and Learning Science with Young Children

The dawn of the twenty-first century finds science curricula strongly influenced by two factors: an emphasis on scientific literacy (American Association for the Advancement of Science 1993; Australian Education Council 1994; National Research Council 1996; Millar & Osborne 1998) and the constructivist view of learning (e.g., Driver et al. 1994). Some, however (e.g., Bybee 1993), caution that our optimism in these new perspectives may be misplaced and argue that there is an urgent need to restore confidence in elementary science education and address its problems.

Key issues of concern are teachers' conceptions of science (Hammrich 1998), teachers' confidence and competence to teach the subject (Goodrum, Cousins, & Kinnear 1992), and teachers' attitude toward science education (Coulson 1992). In this chapter, we explore how these concerns can be addressed through inservice and preservice teacher education.

We examine in particular an inservice program for teachers of young children that was novel in two ways. First, a team approach was adopted in the presentation of the program. Early childhood teacher educators and science teacher educators joined forces to give students the benefits of their distinct kinds of expertise, with the early childhood educators presenting the greater part of the program.

Second, feedback from teachers in the inservice program was used to inform changes to the science component of a preservice teacher education program. The rationale behind this approach was that teachers have a wealth of professional experience that can be used to enhance preservice courses.

The status of science education

Simply put, science is currently understood as the study of patterns and relationships in nature (Steen 1994). Although teachers play an important role in the prevailing view, their conceptions of science may be restricted to how they have applied it to their curricula and assessment tasks. Further, they likely are influenced by their own school days, in which the teaching of science was authoritative rather than exploratory.

Indeed, the authoritative approach still prevails in many schools, as evidenced by today's focus on learning scientific facts, many of which are esoteric and soon forgotten. This kind of education has been described as the *Moses model* in which "a patriarch brings down the tablets of stone carrying the eternal verities and the task of the students is to memorize the contents" (Fletcher & Lowe 1993, 21).

An authoritative view of science is unacceptable for three reasons. First, in that model, the students are limited to well-defined problems that can be solved in isolation, and the implications of the solution are generally ignored. In reality, however, problems are almost always ill defined, at least to begin with, and need to be investigated by teams with diverse expertise. Moreover, the implications of the solution must be considered.

Second, the problems of a society, such as pollution, are largely the outcome of the practices of that society. Therefore, scientific literacy is a goal not just for scientists, but for all citizens, so that they may make informed decisions.

Third, a static view of scientific knowledge is inappropriate in a rapidly changing technological society. For example, the widespread usage of electronic fund transfers and the Internet, fueled by advances in computer technology, have created a need for science to address the problem of the security of access to information with more urgency. Thus, science in a technological society is inherently dynamic.

Confidence and competence of teachers of science

Among the many factors identified as contributing to the status quo in science education are teachers' negative attitudes toward science and science teaching. These attitudes include a lack of interest in science (de Laat & Watters 1995), anxiety about science (Watters & Ginns 1994), a lack of confidence and competence to teach science (Goodrum, Cousins, & Kinnear

1992), a lack of commitment to teaching science (Enochs & Riggs 1990), an inadequate background in science (Tilgner 1990), and the avoidance of teaching science (Enochs & Riggs 1990). Not even increased attention to such attitudes has been sufficient to alter classroom practices, which, on the whole, have not changed significantly in at least the past two decades (Tobin, Tippins, & Hook 1993). To alter teachers' beliefs about their ability to teach science, teachers need to have successful experiences teaching the subject.

Preservice teacher education programs in science

The need for reform in science education presents a challenge for teacher educators (Hammrich 1998). Preservice teachers hold a variety of misconceptions about science (Ginns & Watters 1995), their understanding of concepts may be only slightly better than that of the children they teach (Tilgner 1990), and they may not reason at the level required to solve challenging problems (Ginns & Watters 1995). Thus, it may be difficult for them to plan and orchestrate inquiry-based approaches to science (National Research Council 1996).

Within certain groups of preservice students, a limited background is even more prevalent than among the student population as a whole (McCormack 1992). For example, the common explanation for the underrepresentation and underachievement of females in science is that they "do not tinker" or have had fewer opportunities to do so (Parsons 1995, 217). Tinkering plays an important role in developing an understanding of the physical sciences (Parsons 1995). Gender is a particularly significant issue in early childhood education, because it is mainly women who work with young children.

In an effort to address these problems, a number of changes have been made to the science component of preservice teacher education programs. For instance, some universities, including our own, have increased the contact time in science subjects. Other efforts to improve preparation in science education also are under way. With guidance from the literature, we developed an inservice program for early childhood education teachers. Then, using what we had learned from that program, we incorporated its content and approach into a preservice program for teacher educators.

The sections that follow present our experiences with the two programs and draw some conclusions regarding their general applicability.

Project background

For some time in the state of Queensland, Australia, the responsibility for pursuing professional development has been with teachers themselves. The major providers of training, such as the state education system, have reduced professional development opportunities for early childhood education teachers, stating that such development should be undertaken outside teaching hours. In addition, the state education system has limited professional development opportunities by withdrawing early childhood curriculum consultants from teacher education classrooms.

In this context, early childhood education teachers felt a strong need for professional development in science, and in 1993 they raised this need as a priority to their state association. In 1994 a project proposed jointly by the early childhood professional organization and our university received federal funding. The aim of the project was to enhance the learning and teaching of science in the early years of schooling.

The project originally had three objectives. First, it was to assist teachers in broadening and deepening their knowledge of science. Second, it engaged teachers in extending their range of science teaching strategies for young children and, in the process, enhancing their teaching confidence and competence. Finally, the project would contribute to the development, testing, and distribution of a variety of practical resource materials suitable for use in early childhood education classrooms. As a by-product, the program would also encourage participants to network in school communities and regional groups in an effort to enhance the professional culture of teachers.

An inservice program in science education

The inservice program consisted of a total of eight hours of participation on a Friday afternoon and the following Saturday morning. Teachers could participate in a variety of locations throughout the state. A team made up of science teacher educators and early childhood teacher educators presented the program. The early childhood educators were responsible for helping teachers make connections between the science content and the early childhood education curriculum.

The eight-hour inservice program had three components: (a) the science curriculum (Australian Education Council 1994), (b) teaching and learning science in the early childhood years, and (c) hands-on, "minds-on" approaches. Only the last two components are discussed here.

Teaching and learning science in the early childhood years

The early childhood teacher educators introduced the teacher participants to some of the issues brought up in the literature. To demonstrate key elements of effective science teaching and to launch a discussion of those elements, the participants viewed a video (Fleer 1994) that showed a teacher and 5- and 6-year-old children working with batteries and bulbs.

In the social-constructivist approach depicted in the video, it is important for the teacher to find out what the children know about batteries and bulbs at the beginning of the investigation. Once the children have articulated what they know, the teacher works with them to identify the particular areas in which they want to further their understanding about the topic. The teacher then groups the children according to their questions, and in small groups the children decide how the investigation will proceed. When they complete their investigations, the children record their findings and report to the rest of the class. They then reflect on what they have learned and what their next investigation might be.

As inservice participants learn from the video, the teacher's roles are to read about the topic in preparation for the investigation, to organize the resources needed, and to provide strategic scaffolding for the children's investigations. It is also important for the teacher to encourage the children to reflect on what they have understood and achieved after each session.

Following the presentation of the video, the teachers became involved in an in-depth discussion of teaching approaches used in learning science. They analyzed the steps depicted in the video and discussed the organizational strategies and teaching techniques employed in the process of the investigation. The video and the subsequent discussion assisted many teachers in reflecting on their beliefs and practices regarding the teaching of science.

Hands-on, minds-on

Another key component of the inservice training was participants interacting with each other and with a range of materials—investigating concepts relating to matter, sound, magnetism, and electricity. This hands-on, minds-on component is the approach to teaching and learning science that participants saw in the video and discussed after viewing it.

On a given topic—matter, for instance—participants examined and recorded what they already knew. The inservice leader then introduced other concepts and information relevant to the subject at hand. For example, when the topic was the concept of matter, the discussion

included the states of matter—solid, liquid, and gas—density, and surface tension.

The participants then were given the opportunity to make connections between what they already knew—their knowledge of matter that emerged from their earlier examination of the topic—and their subsequent investigations. Following the latter, each participant offered a brief oral reflection about matter, again linking conceptual understandings to the results of their investigations.

After the inservice program, participants completed feedback forms that provided information on what worked and what did not, in order to help design future inservice programs as well as inform the preservice program.

Theoretical framework for the inservice program

The inservice program was informed by three approaches to teaching and learning science.

Science and the world

Science is an important way, although not the only way, to help people understand issues facing them and the world. Leaders of the inservice program acknowledged the value of other ways of interpreting the world, such as explanations from Aboriginal legends. (See, for example, Knudtson & Suzuki 1994.) Likewise, they explicitly noted that the program reflected one particular approach to teaching and learning science that participants might like to consider.

The leaders emphasized the goal of understanding science and scientific principles in everyday life. Toward that end, science needs to be incorporated into both everyday classroom life and the curriculum. Key to this approach is capitalizing on the opportunities for learning about and appreciating science not only in school, but also in the community and in children's home lives.

Constructivism and beyond

Underlying the inservice program was a constructivist approach to teaching and learning science (Driver et al. 1994), in combination with other approaches that foster social and collaborative learning and incorporate issues of social justice. Constructivism emphasizes that knowledge and understanding occur as an individual interacts with objects and events and makes sense of experiences in light of her or his prior knowledge (Tobin 1993; Bereiter 1994; Driver et al. 1994; Cobern 1995). During the inservice program, participants were encouraged to consider where different systems of values are operating, such as in different social, cultural, or geographical contexts, and to examine the different ways of learning that may occur within these contexts. (See, e.g., Knudtson & Suzuki 1994.)

Emphasizing the social and collaborative nature of learning drew on social constructivist approaches (Driver et al. 1994) and incorporated the concept of scaffolding, based on the Vygotskian notion that social interaction and expert guidance facilitate learning (Vygotsky 1978). Scaffolds are "forms of support provided by the teacher (or another student) to help students bridge the gap between their current abilities and the intended goal" (Rosenshine & Meister 1992, 26). They may be verbal cues or prompts (Rosenshine & Meister 1992); they may also be pictorial or textual cues, such as labels (Beck 1991).

Inservice participants learned that expert guidance for children comes from a variety of sources, including teachers, other adults, and knowledgeable classmates, all of whom provide scaffolding through play and interaction.

Tinkering with materials and ideas

Tinkering with materials and ideas, widely recognized as important in developing scientific knowledge (Wasserman 1992), fits well with constructivist and social-constructivist approaches.

Opportunities to tinker with materials and equipment such as batteries and lightbulbs in situations with other learners give young children scope to observe and reflect on the consequences of actions taken, as well as to think about and discuss observations and raise questions that relate to the materials. Effective teachers of science not only provide a supply of engaging, relevant materials, but they also give learners conceptual support. They state what is known; paraphrase, redirect, and question ideas and approaches; provide information for the students' consideration (or arrange for learners to have access to a source that provides information); and assist with problem solving. Tinkering is pivotal to later investigation, as it provides the basis from which children formulate questions and set about finding the answers.

Because early childhood teachers were active participants in the inservice program, they could see for themselves the value of exploring ideas, discussing those ideas with each other, and using the hands-on, minds-on approach. Teachers enjoyed playing around with the resources, trying out their ideas, and modifying the investigations to find out about something else that interested them.

In the final stage of the program, the teachers were reminded of their own enthusiasm and engagement in this active-learning mode and were encouraged to give children similar opportunities to enjoy scientific investigations in a supportive atmosphere. Teachers also were encouraged to network with science educators in the school and scientists in the surrounding community to "pick their brains" for scientific information. Consulting reference books to plan and implement investigations with children was also identified as important.

Two common concerns of teachers

Feedback from the participants in the inservice program identified concerns related to resources and teaching ideas.

Science materials

In the inservice program, many experienced teachers reported that they found teaching science difficult because they lacked equipment and materials suitable for young children. They seemed to think that specialized equipment was necessary for successful science programs.

While this may be the case for some topics, many exciting scientific investigations can be undertaken with materials typically found in the home. Such materials are relatively inexpensive and easily replaced. Most of the materials used in the inservice workshops were of this variety, and teachers saw opportunities for using similar resources with their classes.

Ideas for science investigations

Teachers confessed that they had few ideas about the type of hands-on, minds-on science learning opportunities to provide for young children when they returned to their classrooms. They were willing to involve children in the kind of investigations they themselves had experienced in the workshop, but many felt that they needed further ideas. Numerous resource books are available for teaching science to young children, yet the teachers in the program appeared to lack confidence in using

those resources to find ideas or the answers to questions children might ask.

This concern highlights a general ongoing problem for inservice education programs: however successful a program might be in the short term, teachers feel the need for ongoing classroom support—for their own scientific knowledge and understanding, as well as for effective methods of teaching and learning science.

When we began our inservice program, we were well aware of the limitations of short-term professional development programs. However, the inservice participants' feedback highlighted the importance of teachers feeling confident in their knowledge of science and in knowing where to seek further information. Indeed, the program demonstrated how critical it is to develop such knowledge in preservice programs and beyond.

Learning from the inservice program

As educators involved in ongoing teacher training, we learned a great deal that has been useful in redesigning the early childhood science program for preservice students. This learning has enhanced the quality of the program with respect to its content, science resources, and ideas for science investigations.

Science content

Early childhood teachers and student teachers frequently raise questions about science content and express discomfort with their lack of scientific knowledge. To give students a solid grounding in science, the preservice program now includes readings to increase their scientific knowledge as well as demonstrate how it applies to the curriculum. Early childhood professors relate their lectures and tutorials to the content of specific readings and work to enhance conceptual knowledge and foster a better understanding of teaching approaches.

With regard to assessment, the inservice teachers helped us to see that students need opportunities to demonstrate their scientific knowledge in practical and interactive ways. For example, one assessment task now calls for preservice students to present a group workshop in which participants gain a conceptual understanding of a scientific topic, such as magnetism. Students responsible for the workshop also furnish their peers with a written summary of the content relating to the topic.

The cumulative learning opportunities provided in the workshops, lecture, and tutorial periods, as well as the reading materials, are now more deliberately planned to build a better understanding of science to enable students to teach science effectively and confidently.

Conclusion

Through what we learned from the inservice program, our own team of early childhood teacher educators was able to refine the preservice early childhood science program.

The approach of "working scientifically" was appealing to teachers and students alike. Experience with teachers and teachers-in-training confirmed the need to go beyond the laboratory model that features the science educator, literally or metaphorically dressed in the white laboratory coat, imparting knowledge through structured experiments. That way, science can become a meaningful part of early childhood teachers' lives.

Although the programs described here move toward achieving that aim, they also need to be dynamic, flexible, and sensitive as we respond to the challenge of developing more effective ways to teach and learn science

with young children. Through such inservice and preservice programs, teacher educators can assist practicing and prospective teachers in recognizing the value of three of the four goals for school science articulated by the National Research Council (1996, 13):

1. Experience the richness and excitement of knowing about and understanding the natural world.

2. Use appropriate scientific processes and principles in making personal decisions.

3. Engage intelligently in public discourse and debate about matters of scientific concern.

In sum, reform in science education is possible only if teachers and learners are prepared to "turn the inside out" and critically reflect on their beliefs and practices about science and science teaching. Once their awareness has been raised, teachers have an opportunity to "let the outside in" by being open minded about, and receptive to, curriculum reform and by responding professionally in establishing how such reform can best benefit their students.

References

American Association for the Advancement of Science. 1993. *Benchmarks for scientific literacy.* New York: Oxford University Press.

Australian Education Council. 1994. *A statement on science for Australian schools.* Carlton, Australia: Curriculum Corporation.

Beck, C.R. 1991. Strategies for cueing visual information: Research findings and instructional design implications. *Educational Technology* 24 (3): 16–20.

Bereiter, C. 1994. Constructivism, socioculturalism, and Popper's world 3. *Educational Researcher* 23 (7): 21–23.

Bybee, R.W. 1993. *Reforming science education: Social perspectives and personal reflections.* New York: Teachers College Press.

Cobern, W.W. 1995 Constructivism for science teachers. *Science Education International* 6 (3): 8–12.

Coulson, R. 1992. Development of an instrument for measuring attitudes of early childhood educators towards science. *Research in Science Education* 22: 101–05.

de Laat, J., & J.J. Watters. 1995. Science teaching self-efficacy in a primary school: A case study. *Research in Science Teaching* 25 (4): 453–64.

Driver, R., H. Asoko, J. Leach, E. Mortimer, & P. Scott. 1994. Constructing scientific knowledge in the classroom. *Educational Researcher* 23 (7): 5–12.

Enochs, L.G., & I.M. Riggs. 1990. Further development of an elementary science teaching efficacy instrument: A preservice elementary scale. *School Science and Mathematics* 90 (8): 694–706.

Fleer, M. 1994. *Seeing the light.* Video. Canberra, Australia: University of Canberra.

Fletcher, N., & I. Lowe. 1993. Science education: Contested territory. *EQ Australia* 1: 18–22.

Ginns, I.S., & J.J. Watters. 1995. An analysis of scientific understandings of preservice elementary teacher education students. *Journal of Research in Science Teaching* 32 (2): 205–22.

Goodrum, D., J. Cousins, & A. Kinnear. 1992. The reluctant primary school teacher. *Research in Science Education* 22: 163–69.

Hammrich, P. 1998. What the science standards say: Implications for teacher education. *Journal of Science Teacher Education* 9 (3): 165–86.

Knudtson, P., & D. Suzuki. 1994. *Wisdom of the elders.* St. Leonards, Australia: Allen & Unwin.

McCormack, A.J. 1992. Trends and issues in science curriculum. In *Science curriculum resource handbook: A practical guide for the K–12 curriculum,* eds. D.W. Cheek, R. Briggs, & R.E. Yager, 16–41. Millwood, NY: Kraus International.

Millar, R., & J. Osborne. 1998. *Beyond 2000: Science education for the future.* London: King's College, School of Education.

National Research Council. 1996. *National science education standards.* Washington, DC: National Academy Press.

Parsons, S. 1995. Making sense of students' science: The construction of a model of tinkering. *Research in Science Education* 25 (2): 203–19.

Rosenshine, B., & C. Meister. 1992. The use of scaffolds for teaching higher-level cognitive strategies. *Educational Leadership* 49 (7): 26–33.

Steen, L.A. 1994. Integrating school science and mathematics: Fad or folly? In *A network for integrated science and mathematics teaching and learning plenary papers,* ed. D.F. Berlin. NSF/SSMA Wingspread Conference (Racine, Wisconsin, April 1991). School Science and Mathematics Association. Topics for Teachers Series Number 7. ERIC, ED 376076.

Tilgner, P.J. 1990. Avoiding science in the elementary school. *Science Education* 74: 412–31.

Tobin K., ed. 1993. *The practice of constructivism in science education.* Washington, DC: American Academy of Sciences.

Tobin, K.G., D.J. Tippins, & K. Hook. 1993. Referents for changing a science curriculum: A case study of one teacher's change in beliefs. *Science and Education* (3): 245–64.

Vygotsky, L.S. 1978. *Mind in society: The development of higher psychological processes.* Cambridge, UK: Cambridge University Press.

Wasserman, S. 1992. Serious play in the classroom: How messing around can win you the Nobel Prize. In *Early Childhood Education,* annual ed., 202–08.

Watters, J.J., & I.S. Ginns. 1994. Science anxiety and self efficacy among preservice primary teachers: Origins and remedies. Paper presented at the annual meeting of the Australasian Science Education Research Association, July, in Hobart, Australia.

Preparing Students to Work with Children with Special Needs and Their Families

In most developed countries today, the lives of people with disabilities and their families are very different than in earlier eras when disability was socially unacceptable and individuals who were different were denied participation in everyday social activities (Ashman & Elkins 1998). Disability was hidden from, and ignored by, the wider community. Gradually, with greater social acceptance of disability, identifying and assessing the extent of a person's disability became increasingly important following World War II.

The strong focus on assessment resulted in putting individuals with disabilities in special programs and treatments, separate from the mainstream. Such segregation, however, ignored many of the needs—as well as the personal dignity—of those with disabilities. Rigid compensatory programs for "developmentally deficient" persons contributed further to highlighting differences and segregation, rather than accepting those with disabilities and including them in the community.

The transition from segregation to inclusion gradually gained ground in the 1970s and was influenced by two major forces. First, the families of people with disabilities demanded for them complete social inclusion in education and the wider community. The impetus for this was directly related to an increasing awareness of social justice and the promotion of human rights issues in the latter parts of the 1970s and throughout the 1980s. And second, Western governments began to realize that the overall cost of segregated education was a financial burden on the public purse and that inclusive education, health, and community services represented significant savings.

Under the banner of *social inclusion for all*, segregated services for children with moderate disabilities began disappearing in the 1980s, a move that was initially welcomed enthusiastically by people with disabilities and especially by their families, who had fought and lobbied for the change. Eventually, however, many individuals with disabilities and their families began to realize that, in an attempt to embrace social justice and inclusiveness, some important educational aspects had been lost. Many excellent services had disappeared, and, moreover, choices were no longer available for those who had previously benefited from useful and appropriate segregated services.

Children who have special needs are not only those identified as having disabilities; also included in this category are those who are at risk through health problems, abuse, poverty, and many other conditions that place young children at a disadvantage in the larger society. Some of these children may have developmental problems and disabilities that have not yet been identified. Children who do not have specific disabling conditions but nonetheless have significant special needs, may be considered environmentally deprived.

While early intervention services for young children were designed originally for children with disabilities, they have been extended to a wide range of children at risk for difficulties in school and other settings. Providing programs for those children and families requires professionals to be sensitive and understanding as well as patient; a diagnosis is not always available or easy to make.

The role of the early childhood professional

Contemporary early childhood professionals interact with children with disabilities and their families in the context of providing inclusive services. As reflective practitioners, early childhood educators embrace a philosophy of active learning, inquiry, and problem solving, operating within a climate of high professional standards. This philosophy enables them to implement individualized programs.

Vygotskian (1978) theory acknowledges that learners—for our purposes, preservice students—bring their personal and social orientations, as well as their knowledge and ideas, to their learning experiences. Their backgrounds influence their responses to issues such as human dignity and the individual's right to participate in society. It is important that students' backgrounds, preconceptions, and biases not reduce their effectiveness in communicating and working in partnership with parents.

As a result of their developmental approach to teaching and learning, early childhood teachers are ideally placed to teach young children with a wide range of special needs, including specific disabilities. In practicing this approach, teachers recognize likeness and value difference, an ideal tenet for including children with special needs in early childhood programs. Nevertheless, anxiety and, at times, fear may accompany responses to these children when teachers have little or no experience with, or knowledge about, particular disabling conditions. Accordingly, these negative reactions must be addressed before early childhood education professionals have contact with children and their families.

Conscientious early childhood professionals may perceive themselves as being responsible for "having all the answers" when it comes to the education of young children. That is, they may assume the role of professional expert to the extent that it hinders their communication with parents, who are the real experts about their children—especially parents of children with special needs. Early childhood professionals, particularly at the beginning of their career when they are inexperienced, often are unaware of their inappropriate interactions with parents who have children with disabilities. They may feel threatened by parents' demands and their own lack of experience.

The parents, however, tend to see the situation differently. The following quote from an interview with a mother who has a daughter with spina bifida illustrates the tension that may arise in parent-professional relationships:

Well, that teacher thought she knew it all. I could see that she hated me and my presence in the classroom. But I was just not ready to leave [Susan] in her care—you see, I had this feeling that she was scared of Susan. . . . You know, it was important that Susan was toileted at a specific time—this was essential for her health. But [the teacher] did not see it that way and thought I was fussing about nothing. She said, "Look, just leave her with me. She'll be fine. I had kids like her before. You don't need to tell me how to teach." I was fuming and I wanted to change preschools, but hubby wouldn't let me; he said [to] put up with it, [because] teachers are all the same!

Parents frequently perceive a disproportionate power relationship between themselves and the teacher or administrator. If this perception is not addressed at the beginning of a working relationship, it may result in poor communication and misunderstanding and may harm the parent-professional relationship, to the detriment of the child.

Working together with families who have children with disabilities requires a high degree of professionalism from teachers—professionalism characterized not only by knowledge and an understanding of practice but, most important, by effective communication. Professionalism does not set teachers apart or above; rather, the epithet *professional* implies that teachers are competent in working as partners with the parents and caregivers of children who have disabilities. A professional approach embraces understanding, empathy, and acceptance of the family's values, knowledge, and expertise about their child's disability, together with support and guidance when required.

Building a foundation for working with children and families

Early childhood professionals are committed to a philosophy of supporting children's individual development and learning through individualized programs—a philosophy that extends to children who have special needs. In such cases, three major requirements need to be considered: a sound knowledge of the clinical and environmental issues relevant to specific disabilities; compassion for, and understanding of, family issues; and the ability to share these effectively with parents.

With a foundation in knowledge and compassion and the skill to communicate effectively, students can gain the ability to design and implement individualized programs in consultation with parents and other professionals. These requirements entail a flexible approach to learning, which is, of course, the cornerstone of sound early childhood education.

Etiology of disabilities and special needs

Disability is a complex issue that may be viewed from a single or from multiple perspectives. A disability affects not only the individual, but touches also the family, a range of professionals (e.g., in education, health, and welfare), and the wider community.

No longer are colloquial descriptions such as *mongoloid* for Down syndrome, *spastic* for cerebral palsy or spina bifida, *deaf* for hearing loss, and *blind* as a collective term for all those who are visually impaired acceptable terminology for referring to those disabilities. Whereas knowledge about children's disabilities was once the possession only of medical practitioners and other related academic professionals, today's families and parents tend to be very well informed.

Because early childhood teachers are likely to be the first educators with whom parents come in contact, it is important that these professionals be at least as well informed as the parents in order to participate in an effective exchange of information. Furthermore, in-depth knowledge about particular disabilities allows early childhood professionals to make informed decisions regarding teaching and learning.

How, then, can preservice students best be prepared for teaching children with a wide range of disabilities in contemporary classrooms?

Classroom lectures and practicum. Although courses of study should begin by introducing the characteristics, etiology, incidence, and treatments for the most prominent disabilities, it is unrealistic—and, indeed,

Seeing the Child in Context

Children with special needs, indeed, any children, must be seen in the context of their environments—their families, schools, neighborhoods, communities, and the wider society (Dunst & Trivette 1990; Hayes 1998). This ecological framework was originally proposed by Bronfenbrenner (1977) in the form of a set of interrelated social ecological systems centering on the child, which he identified as micro-, macro-, and mesosystems.

Microsystem. At the microsystem level we consider the child himself. What are the child's needs? What is the nature of the child's disability? To understand and interact with children with special needs, early childhood educators need a sound introduction to the clinical features of the most prevalent disabilities, becoming familiar with the nature, etiology, progression, and limitations of the specific disabilities of the children they will teach. But more important is consideration of the individual ways in which each child experiences the particular disability, as well as acknowledging the child's strengths and abilities.

Mesosystem. The mesosystem consists of the child's immediate and extended family. How do family members interact with the child and with one another? How do they view his disability? Who cares for the child and makes decisions affecting him? What can the family tell the early childhood pro-

fessional about the child's history, current abilities, and special needs? Early childhood education professionals must be willing and able to work in partnership with families to make decisions about the development and learning of children with special needs. And the families of disabled children must understand and take responsibility for the learning process, which involves shared experiences between children, parents, and early childhood and associated professionals.

Macrosystem. Finally, at the macrosystem level we consider the child's neighborhood, school, and wider community, as well as relevant professionals and support agencies. How does the child fit in with his surroundings? What social challenges does the child face, and how might the early childhood professional help the child meet them? Adapting early childhood curricula to inclusive settings and designing individualized programs requires an awareness of the wider community. Specific social and cultural factors—for example, socioeconomic status or ethnicity—influence the child and require the early childhood professional to adapt the curriculum accordingly.

Each child, with or without special needs, exists at the intersection of these three systems. To work effectively with the child, the early childhood educator must grasp the complex web of relationships and influences that comprise the child's worldview.

counterproductive—to expect preservice students to become experts in all facets of disabilities. Students usually have not had much contact with children with disabilities, so specific conditions are of an abstract nature to them. Because individuals find it more difficult to learn and relate to subjects that they have encountered only in the abstract, having preservice

students absorb clinical details of a disability such as Down syndrome or cerebral palsy may be an exercise in futility.

Students should be introduced in a practical way to information about disabilities, by allowing them to make their own observations during their practicum periods. Once students actually interact with a child with a disability, their interest level and ability to learn are likely to increase significantly.

For example, an instructor may choose to introduce students to Down syndrome, a chromosomal abnormality that occurs in about 1 in 800 live births (Bell 1991), recognizing that students are likely to encounter children with Down syndrome in their work. Although lectures, tapes, handouts, and textbooks are useful in imparting specific information about such a condition, individuals are far more motivated to acquire this knowledge if they have experience with a child who has Down syndrome and the child's family.

Audiovisuals. Audiovisual aids are a useful teaching tool, provided that the information is presented in the proper context and serves the purpose of the discussion at hand. The material should be viewed by small groups, rather than shown in a large lecture hall. In that way, various issues can be identified and openly discussed, which creates an environment more conducive to individual learning.

Meeting with parents who have children with disabilities can reinforce the audiovisual material and place it in a practical context. The opportunity to interact with experienced teachers who can discuss the information presented is invaluable.

Research. Preservice students may not meet a child with a particular disability for some years after they graduate and by then may have forgotten details of the disability learned during their preprofessional course of study. It is important, therefore, that students have the skills to locate the most current information as they need it. Toward that end, imparting research skills becomes an important part of the curriculum for preservice early childhood education students.

Partnerships with families

Henry (1997) notes and examines the importance of maintaining a working relationship between children, early childhood profession-als, and parents. She specifically discusses the triangular relationship between early childhood professionals and parents of children with disabilities.

How can educators prepare students to be effective partners with parents?

Respect for families. At the outset, it is important to convey to students the fact that families who have a child with special needs are not functionally different from other families. In past decades, psychologists tended to view such families as different from other families; they were even perceived as pathological (see, for example, Crnic, Friedrich, & Greenberg 1983). Later research strongly suggests that the presence of a disability, while certainly placing additional stress on family functioning, does not automatically result in pathology (Mahoney, O'Sullivan, & Robinson 1992; Bower 1997).

To seek homogeneity in family functioning is unrealistic and stems from a pervasive tendency of the human sciences to generalize (Hayes & Gunn 1991). Early childhood education students must view families with a child with special needs as functional, unless there are specific indicators to the contrary.

Certain needs are basic to all families seeking professional help: they want assurance that they are receiving the most appropriate services for their children. Furthermore, parents want to have confidence in those who work with their children.

It is essential that teachers convey respect, knowledgeability, and compassion because, by the time parents of children with special needs have their first contact with early childhood education teachers, they have had many diverse experiences, both positive and negative, with a range of professionals. Education, health, and welfare programs for children with disabilities fail to be fully effective if parent-professional relationships are less than optimal.

In sum, parents need to be recognized as caring and intelligent individuals who have the ability and the right to participate in decisionmaking, while at the same time looking for guidance and support from early childhood professionals.

The grieving process. Parents who have a child with a disability may undergo a grieving process not unlike the emotional reactions of parents to the loss of a child through death (Kuebler-Ross 1969). In both cases, the grieving period often extends for a longer time than families expect. The process is highly individual and varies among families. While some individuals and families come to terms with the situation in a relatively short time frame, the grieving of others remains a lifelong process, with a degree of ebb and flow.

While early childhood education teachers are not expected to become counselors for such parents—and indeed, are advised not to do so—they need to understand the grieving process; they must be supportive and compassionate without becoming personally involved. This is a difficult task for young and relatively inexperienced professionals, and adequate preparation for it during professional study is essential.

Cook, Tessier, and Klein (1996) suggest that Kuebler-Ross's classic five stage grieving process (1969) relates to the grieving parent of a child with a disability as follows.

1. Shock, disbelief, and denial. Parents feel shame, guilt, and unworthiness, and therefore overcompensate for these emotions. They may consult physician after physician, searching for a more palatable diagnosis.

2. Anger and resentment. Parents transfer their anger to the center, verbally abusing the early interventionist caring for their child.

3. Bargaining. Working with determination, parents postpone intellectual acceptance of the inevitable.

4. Depression and discouragement. Parents feel helpless, asking "What's the use?" Parents mourn the loss of the image of a "normal" child.

5. Acceptance. Parents realize that something can be done, and adjust their lifestyles accordingly. They are willing to act practically.

Cook and colleagues (1996) suggest that early childhood professionals can meet parents' needs by responding to all five stages of their grieving. Their model serves as an effective teaching tool for introducing early childhood preservice students to this highly sensitive and personal process. Responses such as denial, anger, bargaining, and discouragement are all detrimental to a prospective teacher–parent relationship and have the potential to become a destructive element in the communication process between teacher and parent. Preservice students need to learn not only understanding but acceptance of parental reactions.

Communication with families

Effective communication between families and professionals is based on trust. Without trust, teachers are powerless to facilitate problem solving or create effective education and service plans for families and children. How can preservice students learn the communication skills necessary to become effective partners with families?

Learning through role play. Communication skills can be introduced through lecture and discussion, but they then need to be practiced. Role play, combined with open discussions of emotive responses and reactions, offers an excellent forum for practicing.

Many students initially dislike role play, because they feel personally exposed (Bower 1992). All students, however, need to practice communication skills, and role play represents an important and valuable learning experience for them. My teaching experience has shown that students ultimately agree that role-playing significantly helps them to develop effective skills for communicating with parents.

Prior to students' initial experience with role play, it is useful to find out their feelings about communicating with parents, including instances when a conflict or problem exists. Students are encouraged to assess themselves as communicators by formally identifying their strengths and weaknesses. Students' nervousness about role-playing, they are reminded, may be likened to the anxiety and discomfort many parents experience when they first interact with professionals. This awareness may promote empathy in future encounters with parents.

The initial session serves as an icebreaker and may help students to participate in role playing. Grouping students in threes allows them to take turns in the roles of parent, teacher, and observer. The purpose of the observer is to give feedback to the two communicating participants—a valuable learning experience in itself.

While students are encouraged to use their individual experiences in role play, it is wise to provide them with short scripts they can initially use. Here are two sample scenarios that describe a potentially difficult situation for a teacher:

> I feel that my child is not included in all the activities that other children participate in. She seems to be an outsider, and my husband and I feel that she is treated differently from other children.

> You professional people expect so much from us parents. If I were to act on all of your suggestions—all the things I should do with Jason to improve his development—I would not have time to be a wife and mother . . . you are quite unrealistic; there is only so much one person can do. And I send him to preschool so that you can do your job as a teacher and I do mine as a mother.

It is of utmost importance that students realize that they do not have to provide answers to everything and solve parents' every problem. Early childhood professionals just need to listen to parents and make them feel that they understand. (We say *just,* but it is a big *just.*)

The teacher's responsibility lies in facilitating the problem-solving process for parents, perhaps by encouraging parents to consider different viewpoints. Teachers also should provide some factual information and suggest various resources. Communicating with parents is thus a process-oriented, multidimensional activity and does not necessarily have to be content based (Henry 1997).

For students to become confident in their communication abilities, it is important that they have opportunities to practice over time. Each student should assume the roles of parent, teacher, and observer as many times as possible. Once their communication skills become more integrated, the students can use them more readily in real-life situations.

Through the years, I have had much positive feedback from students who initially approached role-playing with trepidation and skepticism but later progressed to active learning and increased communication skills.

Effective interviewing. Early childhood teachers need sound interviewing skills. Parents will trust teachers and share important information with them if the parents believe that the teachers are interviewing them fairly. To gain parents' trust, teachers must go beyond merely asking the parents a series of questions; instead, they need to encourage the parents to respond in the context of their own experiences.

Social scientists have identified a genuine interest in others as a major requirement for a successful interview (Babbie 1992; Bower 1997). However, Seidman (1991) warns of the risks of overfamiliarity, while McCracken (1988) suggests that interviewers who ignore contextual awareness may spark resentment in interviewees, leading them to terminate the interview. Bower (1997) proposes that, for the purpose of eliciting parents' real opinions and feelings, interviewers should never pose direct questions (except to obtain data) but instead should invite parents to talk about specific topics. Parents then can present their own views and experiences if they so desire.

To learn interviewing skills, students may first prepare their own interview protocol focusing on a specific topic. They will refine this on the basis of feedback from fellow students and instructors. They then are ready to try out their protocol with parents who volunteer to participate.

Taping the interview, with parents' permission, is valuable for students in debriefing and honing their protocol and skills. Students are strongly advised not to interview relatives or close friends, as such relationships significantly alter the interviewer-interviewee dynamics.

Individual education plans and individual family service plans

Individual education plans and individual family service plans are the basis for providing meaningful programs for children with special needs, and they furnish the link between communication with parents and the implementation of curriculum. The purpose of teachers' involvement in these plans is fully described in other literature (Allen & Schwartz 1996; Cook, Tessier, & Klein 1996). Suffice it to say here that good communication skills in general, and good interviewing skills in particular, can greatly facilitate formulating individual education plans and individual family service plans.

Early childhood teachers are skilled in individualizing programs for young children because of their belief that children's development is highly individualized. Yet the commitment to this philosophy may prevent preservice students and teachers from including children with special needs in the activities of other children. Students need to understand that a truly inclusive program allows all children, including children with special needs, to use their existing skills, be they social, cognitive, or physical, and learn new ones.

Early childhood teacher educators need to use practical, generic instructional strategies that can provide preservice students with the methodological basis for intervention programs for all children.

Videotapes and discussion. The use of videotapes, followed by small-group discussions, can be an effective way to introduce students to the notion of all children using their existing skills and developing new ones. I typically use two video segments.

The first is a scenario portraying a segregated educational setting using a highly struc-

tured, typically behaviorist approach to task analysis and reinforcement strategies. The second video shows a more contemporary approach, geared toward using individualized skills in inclusive settings. Here, children with disabilities are included in the same activities as other children, yet specific skills are taught individually, and tasks and expectations are highly individualized. Students viewing the videos are encouraged to identify the significant issues and discuss the advantages and disadvantages of the two methods.

Small-group discussions are ideal for this task, and students are encouraged to write curricula for children with special needs, based on the students' observations during real-life practicum situations or in response to written examples. The curricula are then evaluated in a large-group discussion, and suggestions for amending the programs are implemented. The university teacher then constructively criticizes students' proposals, thereby ensuring that unthought-of aspects of individualized planning have been considered.

Although training videos are generally widely available from university libraries, instructors may wish to produce video segments for their own teaching purposes, as I myself have done.

Practicum. After classroom instruction using videotapes, the students can plan, implement, and evaluate a curriculum for a child with a disability in a practicum situation. This final task is linked to the assessment program for the course, which is discussed next.

Assessment as a learning experience. The assessment process meets the requirements of the university in terms of ascertaining that students who have studied a particular unit have acquired the knowledge and skills relevant to the material studied.

Assessing student comprehension via examinations can provide opportunities in the learning process, but students learn little from answering a large number of multiple-choice questions spread over a wide range of topics at the end of the course. Through short essay questions at the end of specific segments of the course, students can demonstrate their in-depth understanding of the subject.

Researching topics of their choice in the area of disability and carrying out relevant fieldwork using observation and written and oral reports to fellow students help students expand and consolidate their knowledge and skills.

Student assessment in a course has both practical and theoretical components. The practical components can be assessed on a satisfactory/unsatisfactory basis and involve students' participation in role-playing and written self-evaluations of their individual progress, difficulties, and achievements in this area.

Assessment of theoretical components requires students to work with a child with special needs in an early childhood setting of their choice. Students must briefly review the literature on the specific special needs of that child, indicating their full understanding of the issues. The students then negotiate with the child's parents for permission to observe the child in a chosen setting. In consultation with the child's teacher, they prepare a meaningful observation schedule for a minimum of three sessions.

The final requirement for the theoretical component is for students to interview the child's parents, after which students draw up a plan on a number of topics relating to parents' experiences with children with disabilities. In this task, students are required to demonstrate both understanding and skills they have acquired during their course of study. Finally, they present their findings in a written report.

In addition to helping instructors evaluate students, assessments provide university teachers with important feedback about the effectiveness of the material they have presented and the teaching methods they have used.

In sum, all assessment activities should be both a learning experience and a demonstration of knowledge and skills acquired in the course.

Conclusion

Teaching young children with disabilities is a multifaceted experience that goes beyond designing individualized programs for the children to encompassing the involvement of parents and other professionals. Early childhood education professionals can no longer expect special education teachers to undertake this duty, since the practice of mainstreaming children with disabilities has become common. It is now important that *all* early childhood education professionals—not only special education teachers—have the knowledge, understanding, and skills necessary to teach these children and to interact with other professionals and the children's parents.

This chapter examined some ways in which preservice early childhood education students can become knowledgable, skillful, and comfortable in working with children with special needs and their families. An integrated teaching approach grounded in early childhood philosophy and practice can prepare preservice students for the sensitive task of including these children in the classroom.

There are, of course, limitations in the approach described, not the least of which is time. Certainly, preservice students do not come out of their course of study as experienced practitioners. However, the combination of relevant information, practical involvement, improved communication skills, and problem solving that they receive forms a basis for increased confidence in their ability to be successful in their practice of teaching and communicating with children and families affected by disability or special needs.

Finally, students are most likely to practice their newly gained skills if they feel that the teaching phase has been interesting, enjoyable, and relevant. Faculty need to retain their flexibility, openness, and sense of humor as they put into practice the teaching approaches discussed here.

References

Allen, K.E., & I.S. Schwartz. 1996. *The exceptional child: Inclusion in early childhood education.* Albany, NY: Delmar.

Ashman, A., & J. Elkins. 1998. *Educating children with special needs.* 3d ed. Sydney: Prentice Hall.

Babbie, E. 1992. *The practice of social research.* Belmont, CA: Wadsworth.

Bell, J.A. 1991. The epidemiology of Down syndrome. *The Medical Journal of Australia* 155: 115–17.

Bower, A.M. 1992. Acquiring interpersonal communication skills through simulated learning in teacher education. In *Exploring tertiary teaching,* eds. P. Weeks & D. Scott, 99–107. Armidale, Australia: University of New England.

Bower, A.M. 1997. *A comparative study of mothers' beliefs and ideas about mothering in families with and without disability.* Ph.D. diss., University of Queensland, Brisbane, Australia.

Bronfenbrenner, U. 1977. Toward an experimental ecology of human development. *American Psychologist* 32: 513–31.

Cook, R.E., A. Tessier, & M.D. Klein. 1996. *Adapting early childhood curricula for children in inclusive settings.* 4th ed. Englewood Cliffs, NJ: Merrill.

Crnic, K.A., W.N. Friedrich, & M.T. Greenberg. 1983. Adaptation of families with mentally retarded children: A model of stress, coping, and family ecology. *American Journal of Mental Deficiency* 88: 125–38.

Dunst, C.J., & C.M. Trivette. 1990. Assessment of social support in early intervention programs. In *Handbook of early childhood intervention,* eds. S.J. Meisels & J.P. Shonkoff, 326–49. Cambridge, UK: Cambridge University Press.

Hayes, A. 1998. Disabilities and families. In *Educating children with special needs,* 3d edition, eds. A. Ashman & J. Elkins, 38–69. Sydney: Prentice Hall.

Hayes, A., & P. Gunn. 1991. Developmental assumptions about Down syndrome and the myth of uniformity. In *Adolescence with Down syndrome: International perspectives on research and program development. Implications for parents, researchers and practitioners,* ed. C.J. Dunholm, 73–81. Victoria, BC, Canada: University of Victoria.

Henry, M. 1997. *Young children, parents, and professionals: Enhancing the links in early childhood.* London: Routledge.

Kuebler-Ross, E. 1969. *On death and dying.* London: Travstock.

Mahoney, G.O., P. O'Sullivan, & C. Robinson. 1992. Family environments with children with disabilities: Diverse but not so different. *Topics in Early Childhood and Special Education* 12: 386–402.

McCracken, G. 1988. *Qualitative research methods: The long interview.* London: Sage.

Seidman, I.E. 1991. *Interviewing as qualitative research.* New York: Teachers College Press.

Vygotsky, L.S. 1978. *Mind in society: The development of higher psychological processes.* Cambridge, MA: Harvard University Press.

Margaret Henry

Open Doors, Open Minds: Working with Families and Community

Parents bringing their 4-year-olds to preschool in the morning huddle under the eaves as a thundershower breaks over the school building. Looking out at them from her comfortable office is the teacher, who will let them in at precisely nine o'clock. The parents are not even disgruntled; they have come to accept that this is the way things are done.

*N*ot all early childhood programs shut families out like this. In some programs, directors and teachers not only maintain open doors, but work hard at establishing "reciprocal relationships with families" (Bredekamp & Copple 1997, 3). The importance of developing partnerships between educators and the families of the children they serve is not a new idea; it has long been part of the research literature (Gray & Klaus 1965; Schaefer 1968; Bronfenbrenner 1969) and has been increasingly emphasized in recent years (Powell 1989; Davies 1990; Swap 1991; Epstein 1992; Chavkin

1993; Moles 1993; Berger 1995). Building partnerships with families, in fact, is one of the fundamental principles of many early childhood programs today—but not all.

In many programs, such as the one described here, reciprocal relationships with parents are far from being taken for granted. They are *inconceivable*. This chapter discusses why that is so and considers what might be done about it in teacher education programs, using examples from a teacher training course that the author has evolved over a 16-year period.

Families: Are they clients or partners?

As examples of *inappropriate* practices with respect to families, Bredekamp and Copple (1997, 177) list conditions and behaviors such as these:

• School personnel do not involve parents in decisions about how best to handle children's problems or support their learning. They see parents in a negative light, complaining that they have not raised their children well.

• Teachers make only formal contact with parents, through report cards and one yearly conference.

• Schedules are so tight that parents are seen as one more frustration to teachers who need to "cover the curriculum." A policy for parent participation exists, but it receives only lip service.

In programs following these types of practices, the director and teachers see relationships with families as being unimportant and devote very little time to them. Many teacher education courses reflect and contribute to this attitude. As de Acosta (1996) points out, "preservice course work that focuses on what occurs in the classroom leads student teachers to think of teaching as a task accomplished in isolation."

The minuscule amount of attention given to collaboration with families has been documented in the United States by Greenwood and Hickman (1991), who report that less than 2% of competencies measured in state certification of teachers relate to influences outside the classroom. Williams and Chavkin (1987) note that only 4% of teacher training programs devote a whole course to parent involvement, and 37% spend as little as one class period on the topic (de Acosta 1996, 9). Commenting on this "pervasive and amazing omission" from most teacher preparation programs, Greenberg notes: "Very, very few give preservice . . . teachers the amount of history, theory, practice, and sophisticated guidance they need to enable them to work comfortably, extensively, and in a wide variety of ways with *all* kinds of parents" (1989, 67).

The risk of underestimating families

What lies behind the lack of attention many teachers—and many teacher educators—pay to the rest of the child's life? In their first example, Bredekamp and Copple (1997) suggest one aspect of the failure to work closely with families: viewing parents "in a negative light," complaining about their childrearing practices, and blaming them for children's poor school performance. One might, in turn, reflect on whether there lies, behind these attitudes, the propensity of teachers, like other professionals, to behave as colonizers.

Laying claim to parents' territory

Wolfendale (1983) summarizes this view of teachers as colonizers. She notes that parents are seen as being

• like clients, seeking, and depending on, expert help

• passive in receiving services

• in need of redirection

• peripheral to decisionmaking

• inadequate or deficient in certain ways (p.15)

Like the Spanish in South America or the British in India, teachers have moved into an area inhabited by others and claimed the territory. But, unlike local inhabitants who fight back against would-be colonizers, parents seldom offer overt resistance. They are intimidated and see teachers and other professionals as bringing the bounty of expertise —information that parents very much want to have and that teachers and other "experts" may or may not share with them.

Dispensing "expert" advice to parents

This view of parents restricts and distorts the relationship teachers have with them and greatly diminishes the contributions that parents and teachers are able to make to children's and to one another's development and learning. The tendency to underestimate parents is usually based on misperceptions. The box "Some Things Parents Have in Common" (Croft 1979) enumerates parent commonalities, which, if teachers more widely recognized and better understood them, could lead to better parent-teacher relations.

An example of what happens when professionals approach parents with a patronizing

Some Things Parents Have in Common

Although parents' lives are quite varied, they have some important things in common:

1. Parents look to the school and depend heavily upon its staff to maintain the health and emotional well-being of their children.

2. Their training and ideas about raising children may be quite different from the teacher's.

3. They probably feel some sense of guilt or ambivalence about leaving their children in an institution (i.e., child care center, public school).

4. They worry about their children.

5. They hope the teachers relate to their children in a warm and caring way.

6. They are happy to provide input into decision making if they are convinced of the importance of their involvement.

7. Their ideas about the kind of role the teacher should fill are colored by their past experiences with teachers.

8. Their own roles and responsibilities as parents may not be clear to them or to the teacher.

9. Parents come from different backgrounds and have differing needs, so the teacher has to be flexible in methods used to communicate with them.

10. Parents expect teachers to have the expertise to help them raise their children.

11. Parents are more likely to respect the advice of teachers if parents are convinced that the teacher truly cares about the child.

12. Parents are a teacher's most important resource in reinforcing what the school wants the children to learn.

Source: From D. Croft, *Parents and Teachers,* 1st edition. © 1979. Reprinted with permission of Wadsworth, a division of Thomson Learning, fax 800-730-2215.

attitude regarding children's behaviors is an early intervention program in Great Britain (James 1975). Four-year-olds from families with low incomes received regular home visits that attempted to direct the children toward school learning by enlisting the aid of the parents. The format incorporated the use of "parental tasks":

> The technique of introducing "parental tasks" . . . persisted . . . for some time [under] several different formats. Sometimes new ideas would be introduced, [and] sometimes a continuation of the session's activity would be suggested. It must be admitted, however, that little enthusiasm could be raised from visitor or parents about continuing the types of activity through to other times in the week on the parents' initiative. Indeed, a good deal of difficulty was found in involving the mothers during the session. (James 1975, 29)

Ironically, program evaluators found that any gains in parents' attitudes and children's test scores occurred in the control group rather than the intervention group.

A program established in the 1980s to train British health visitors to act as teachers of behavior management (Stevenson, Bailey, & Simpson 1988) recorded similar results. Mothers who expressed difficulty coping with their child's behavior were regularly visited by trained health visitors over a six-month period. Visitors advised the mothers on the use of specific behavior management techniques. The results showed that mothers achieved no significant improvement in coping and that some were "less effective in producing change after being trained" in behavior management (Stevenson, Bailey, & Simpson 1988, 133).

Reporting on the discouraging results of this didactic approach to giving professional advice, the authors disconsolately wondered, "What procedures for the delivery of health visitor expertise can facilitate their effectiveness?" (Stevenson, Bailey, & Simpson 1988, 135).

The form of the question may foreshadow the answer: the "delivery of health visitor expertise," like the "technique of introducing 'parental tasks,'" may never be effective. Parents are not mailboxes to which professionals can deliver expertise or introduce tasks. Parents who are treated, in Wolfendale's (1983) words, as dependent, passive, in need of redirection, peripheral to decisionmaking, inadequate, and deficient are naturally loath to cooperate with those who treat them that way. Unfortunately, the inclination for professionals to approach parents in this manner continues to the present day.

Connecting with parents as partners

Parents need specific information about what is happening in their children's education, but conveying such information is likely to become, for teachers, a one-way transmission. However benign the information the teachers bear, it carries with it the strong scent of authority. Many parents perceive teacher-parent communication as someone directing them as to what is expected of them and their children. Some may harbor resentment, anxieties, and a sense of inadequacy from their own experiences with teachers and schools when they were children. How do we find our way out of this conundrum?

Establishing two-way communication

The only way out is to abandon one-way communication and replace it with reciprocal communication (see "Communicating with Families"). Two-way communication means not only do teachers give something valuable to parents, but parents also give something valuable to teachers. When mutual sharing occurs, teachers are no longer colonizers, and parents need no longer resent what teachers have to give. They become genuine partners.

Recognizing parent strengths and abilities

In the partner approach, parents (1) are active in and central to making and implementing decisions; (2) are seen as having strengths

Communicating with Families

Today's teacher has many constraints to overcome in working with busy parents. The hectic pace of living leaves little time for many adults to attend meetings or volunteer in the classroom. Yet, when parents feel they are partners in their children's program, they are its most loyal supporters. The wise teacher learns how to communicate with parents to involve them in meaningful ways.

There are various methods a teacher can use to communicate the genuine desire for parent participation. The teacher can

• design projects that get children interested in involving their parents.

• build the program, in which parents are expected to participate, around the immediate concerns and lives of the families.

• use every opportunity to build trust and open communication. Sometimes a few words at the door when a parent drops off a child are sufficient to open up more important discussions later on. Smiles, a comforting phrase, a positive comment—all go a long way in building good feelings about the school. Parents are less reluctant to "bother" a teacher if they know the teacher is accepting and receptive.

• let parents know about specific needs, such as seeking volunteers for a field trip, both through general calls for help and by asking particular people to do specific tasks ("I noticed on your forms that you have a very clear style of printing. I wonder if you would be willing to print some of the notices for us from time to time?").

• be sensitive to all parents. Some may require more of your attention, but others who are less demanding of your time also appreciate having you notice them.

• take parents' schedules and constraints into account in planning meetings. For example, it is easier to involve parents when meetings are held in familiar settings close to their homes.

• provide "escape hatches" for parents who do not like to work with children or do not have time to be at the school. Possibilities include working on materials at home, helping with special trips or school events, participating in weekend work to improve the playground or classroom, making phone calls, and addressing letters.

• phone parents during the evening or at other times when they are least likely to be busy. Share some positive anecdote with them about their child, or let them know about some interesting incident that occurred during the day. Or send home a short, friendly note.

• rely on well-established neighborhood groups and institutions like churches and other schools to help bridge the gap between a new program and the home.

• identify genuine needs of the program as opposed to "busy work." Parents are more likely to want to involve themselves in helping to meet genuine needs.

• plan an environment that allows parents to be "experts." If materials are set up in such a way that parents have to ask the teacher every time they need to find something or do a particular task, parents feel less confident about their own abilities.

• describe clearly the goals of the program and show how parent involvement can be of real help.

• provide research results indicating the value of parent involvement in short, easy-to-understand summaries in a newsletter.

• give appreciation and recognition for contributions of time and talent as reinforcement for further parent involvement. Even the smallest act of a parent should be appropriately recognized.

• persist with efforts to communicate. Most parents read the notes that are sent home with the child or pinned to his jacket. They may not respond to these notes as wholeheartedly as the teacher would like, but each note increases their awareness of what the school is doing.

Source: From D. Croft, *Parents and Teachers*, 1st edition. © 1979. Reprinted with permission of Wadsworth, a division of Thomson Learning, fax 800-730-2215.

and expertise equal to those of teachers; (3) contribute, as well as receive, information; and (4) share responsibility with teachers—that is, the parent and teacher are each accountable to the other (Wolfendale 1983).

It is not surprising that teachers often fail to see these capabilities in parents. Parents' sense of intimidation and resentment frequently prevents them from presenting themselves as active, strong, and knowledgeable. "Toward Meaningful Connections with Families" (pp. 110–11) summarizes the conditions and provisions that enable early childhood professionals to develop such relationships with parents.

A course fostering a new attitude

To help teachers and parents enrich their related repertoires, a teacher preparation course must include intensive practice and many opportunities to reflect on and analyze the building of reciprocal relationships. At Queensland University of Technology, a 12-week course called Working with Parents and Community is part of the curriculum.

As a key part of the course, each student meets one child's parent or parents and has the opportunity to work with them. In addition, the student develops an activity for a group of parents, typically related to the special challenges or circumstances of the family they have come to know. When the student shares these experiences and learning with the instructor and fellow students (with the family remaining unidentified, of course), all students gain wider and deeper experience with respect to families. In assignments, each student analyzes the individual project and the group activity, using a framework that incorporates the interlocking needs of children, parents, and professionals and promotes the expansion of resources for all three.

Students come to experiences in working and training with parents and community at different stages in their careers and from varying locations and backgrounds. Preservice or inservice preparation should take these differences into account, and in our course on working with

The task of reweaving parents into the life of an early childhood program requires conceptual and structural provisions that enable all staff to maintain meaningful connections with families.

• *Early childhood programs serve families, not children alone.* All policies and practices, no matter how large or small, should undergo a two-part family impact test: How does this policy or practice affect families? How does this policy or practice genuinely incorporate information from, or the direct involvement of, family members?

• *Program practices in relating to parents must be in tune with widespread demographic trends, especially the characteristics and circumstances of families served by the program.* Methods of working with parents should be locally grown and shaped by the expressed preferences and needs of families. One size does not fit all. Programs need staff who speak the language of the families served, and all staff need a respectful understanding of the values and traditions represented among families.

• *Parent and teacher confidence in each other is the foundation of healthy relationships.* Parents want firm assurances that child care providers and teachers are skilled, knowledgeable, caring individuals. Are there varied and frequent opportunities for parents to get to know staff? Staff training should help strengthen skills in taking family perspectives and identifying parent strengths.

• *Relations with parents should be individualized in a way that informs staff understandings of and work with each child.* Communication must be frequent, personal, and consistent and conducted by the child's primary caregiver or teacher. What type and number of staff are available when parents are most likely to be present, especially at drop-off and pickup times? Is there assignment of a primary teacher who knows the child well and takes responsibility for daily communication with parents? There is great potential in developing or using tools that systematically lead to shared parent-staff goals for a child (for an example, see Murphy 1997). The development of shared goals helps staff understand and respect each child's family and contributes to staff confidence in the parent because there is agreement on program practices.

• *Programs should actively acknowledge parents as persons.* Many roles and aspects of daily life influence parenting. Model programs offer innovative ways for early childhood programs to address a range of adult interests, especially when parents define their own needs. For ex-

parents and community, we strive to do so. For all students in the course, the core goal is fostering more mutually supportive teacher-parent and teacher-family-community relationships by

• deepening students' theoretical understanding of the part parents and other family members play in children's development and the roles they can play in early childhood programs,

• extending students' practical ability to relate to parents and to involve family members in a variety of program approaches, and

• enabling students to identify and draw on community resources and to help families make use of such resources.

Three dimensions of adult behavior

To analyze what is involved in relationships with parents, a model of adult caregiving behavior is useful. The model presented on page 114 (Henry 1996) is derived from the literature (Hess 1971; Gordon 1972; Amato 1987; Ochiltree & Edgar 1995), and it identifies key dimensions of parent behavior in the earliest years of childhood ample, how might staff views of parents be affected if staff were encouraged to find alternatives to referring to a particular parent as someone's mother or father?

• *Parent beliefs may be as important as basic supports are in facilitating parent participation in meetings and other activities.* Basic supports such as child care are essential for enabling parent participation in meetings. Research suggests that also central to parents' decisions about participation are beliefs about their parenting roles, the chances of having a positive impact on their child's education, and perceptions of whether a program is interested in their involvement. What sincere and clear messages do programs give to parents about the role they play in their child's life and in the life of their child's early childhood program?

• *Definitions and assessments of the quality of an early childhood program need to give greater attention to parent perspectives and to program practices with parents and families.* Existing definitions of quality were developed with little regard for parent perspectives (Larner 1996), and widely used tools for assessing program quality give scant attention to relations with parents (Raab & Dunst 1997). Parents consider how an early childhood program *arrangement* will mesh with family life and resources; their

concerns encompass a broader set of considerations than are typically included in quality criteria focused on the program *setting*.

• *Professional education and credentials should promote skills in relating to parents.* The currently weak attention to teachers' demonstrated skills in relating to parents must be strengthened in professional education and state certification requirements. It appears that, among the many competencies required for effective work with parents, special emphasis should be given to skills in learning and appreciating the perspectives of families.

Research suggests that teachers' collaborative relations with parents and work within a family context do not come about naturally or easily. There are numerous challenges at multiple levels. Fortunately, research findings and lessons from model programs offer promising directions for widespread implementation of recommended practices that, in essence, call for a new era in the early childhood field's approaches to families.

Source: Reprinted by permission, with changes, from D.R. Powell, "Research in Review: Reweaving Parents into the Fabric of Early Childhood Programs," *Young Children* 53 (September 1998): 65–66.

that have major facilitating effects on children's personal, social, and cognitive functioning in the first years of school. Henry grouped the parental behaviors identified by Hess (1971) under the following three major dimensions:

• responsiveness, including Hess's parental variables of *warmth, expression of high regard,* and *attentiveness/engagement;*

• control, including Hess's variables of *consistency, explanatory rather than arbitrary regulatory strategies,* and *encouragement of children's independence;* and

• involvement, including Hess's variables of *encouragement of achievement, talking with rather than to, teaching,* and *provision of stimulating resources.*

These dimensions are also evident in the behaviors of family care providers (Henry 1992) and teachers/caregivers in center-based early childhood programs (Clarke-Stewart 1987). Moreover, when participating adults in a variety of parent-professional programs demonstrated the behaviors contributing to responsiveness, mutual control, and involvement in relation to one another, these behaviors accompanied improved relationships and understanding among the adults (Henry 1996).

In learning to build two-way relationships, the students in our parents and community course are strongly encouraged to keep in mind these dimensions of interaction.

Student-family projects

Our students learn to value and develop partnerships with parents through activities in which they engage parents, both singly and in groups. At the beginning of the course, each student approaches the family of a child, and together they identify an area in which either one or both has some concerns about the child. In this process, students become more attentive to parents' ideas and concerns and to what family members are doing to help meet children's needs. They begin to notice the many things that parents do that reflect their caring and responsiveness toward the child.

With such face-to-face experiences, along with classroom discussion, students are less likely to develop the attitude expressed by one teacher, who, watching the children rattling off in the school bus to their families' struggling farms, said, "Those children go home to *nothing!*" On the contrary, students in the course are likely to see parents' strong motivation to contribute to their children's lives and their willingness to try various ideas that the students suggest or that they come up with together.

Collaborating with an individual parent. A student we will call Jeanne observed that a kindergartner, Sarah, seemed to have little interest in identifying letters and words. Approaching Sarah's mother, Candace, in a nonconfrontational, nonjudgmental manner, Jeanne invited her to talk about Sarah's experiences and interests at home and share any of her own ideas and concerns. Jeanne's assignment was to work with the parent to design a cooperative project, building on the child's and parent's interests and addressing a spe-

cific need—in this case, the child's need for literacy experiences in a meaningful, enjoyable context. What Jeanne and Candace devised was a cooking project—making jellied oranges—in which Sarah would help to read the recipe and make the orange treats.

As the student and parent engage the child in their chosen project, each demonstrates his or her own style of control and managing behavior. Students are encouraged to notice parents' behaviors, particularly with respect to the Hess (1971) variables—consistency, explaining to the child (rather than using arbitrary regulating strategies), and encouraging the child's independence. In their own interactions with the child, students try to use this interaction style as well, maintaining an authoritative but not domineering style; taking care to pause, prompt, and praise the child's efforts; and encouraging the child's input.

The participating parent, seeing the efficacy of this approach, often modifies her or his own style to some extent. Although Candace started out using a highly directive approach, she saw that, with Jeanne's prompting and positive feedback, Sarah was able to manage cooking tasks quite successfully. "I've never been game to let her help me in the kitchen," Candace remarked, "but I can see with a bit of time she can do it!"

The project enables the student to build a collaborative relationship with the parent, join the parent in interacting with the child, and gain insights into the life the parent and the child share—all ways of adding to her own and the parents' resources.

Working with a group of parents. As their second course assignment, the students work with parents in groups and, if possible, build on their project with the single family. Jeanne, for example, saw an opportunity to build on her relationship with Candace. Concerned about the unhealthy snacks children were bringing to school, she asked Candace to help conduct a "fun-snack" session for parents and children. Spurred on by the children's eagerness for their parents to learn about the fun-snacks, parents flocked to the meeting. Candace played a major role in the session, and other parents offered ideas, too. Before long, one group of parents began working on a healthy recipe book for young parents like themselves, and another group made a parent video about helping children learn to read from everyday materials such as food packages and junk mail.

Is it safe?

Are there risks in this process? Are inexperienced undergraduates likely to find themselves sucked into difficult or dangerous family situations? In our program, problems of this kind have not occurred. The principal reason, we believe, is that no pressure or dominance is exerted, either by students or parents, within the projects and interactions that comprise much of the course. When people *express* their needs directly rather than relying on inference (Peters & Kostelnik 1981), all participants are able to exchange ideas and learn from one another.

In this context, parents often see students as a source of practical help. "Why is my child so frightened to take the trainer wheels off her bike? Her friend can do it, and she's only six months older." "I want Jake to be sleeping though the night when the new baby arrives, but he keeps getting up and coming into our bed. What do you think we ought to do?" "Now that Hetty's talking, she calls her caregiver 'Mummy,' and I feel a bit left out." Questions such as these from parents raise important developmental issues for students to think and talk about—childhood fears and the growth of trust and autonomy, progression of language skills, and the like. The questions also suggest topics for lively parent-discussion group sessions.

While the faculty involved in this course see undergraduate students as young adults learning to exercise judgment and flexibility, we also recognize that it is essential that students be safe. Students may choose to work on

their skills and understanding with their own relatives who are parents, with families they know well through babysitting, or with families attending the university's toddler center or kindergarten.

Alternatively, with the support of their supervising teacher, students may arrange to interact with parents before or after class at their practice teaching placements. A supportive explanatory letter goes with the students to these placements from the course team members, who are always available to liaise with both students and the center or school.

When students interact with parents in a group, they typically do so with one or two other students, each carrying out different parts of the task. This ensures students' safety and sense of comfort. In some urban areas and other communities with greater safety risks and a greater proportion of families with serious problems, adopting preventive measures of this kind is particularly critical. Faculty may also need to do some preliminary screening of families for participation with students in the course.

Outcomes using this model

What are the outcomes of this model? Research (e.g., Hess 1971) suggests that when adults show behaviors contributing to responsiveness, control, and involvement with children (Henry 1996), the children are more likely to meet the first developmental challenges, identified by Erikson (1950) as the building of trust, autonomy, and initiative. Thus, adult exercise of responsiveness relates to children's development of trust, adult control to children's autonomy, and adult involvement to children's initiative and new ideas.

Turning to the adults—parents and students who participate in this process—we observe the same behavioral dimensions coming into play. When responsiveness, mutual control, and involvement are present, the participating adults are able to show trust, autonomy, and initiative. What all participants gain in such ongoing interaction is shown in the figure, "Three Dimensions of Adult Caregiving Behavior" (see below), which illustrates the model underlying the parent course (Henry 1996).

In this diagram, when the two adults in the parent/professional/child group offer each other, as well as the child, responsiveness, mutual control, and involvement, all three parties are better able to reach out toward trust, autonomy, and initiative (Henry 1996).

The diagram depicts arrows travelling in more than one direction between all the participants; they indicate reciprocal communication. Learning to practice two-way communication through responsiveness, mutual control, and involvement requires time and opportunity. Time and opportunity should be available, both in class and in the field, in preservice or inservice experiences in working with parents. Often, in teacher education courses, they are not. Instead, four or five teachers in a variety of subjects may present isolated aspects of the topic of parent-teacher contact. When this happens, the end product for the student is not an intricate tapestry but small clumps of unconnected threads.

Three Dimensions of Adult Caregiving Behavior and Their Associated Resources

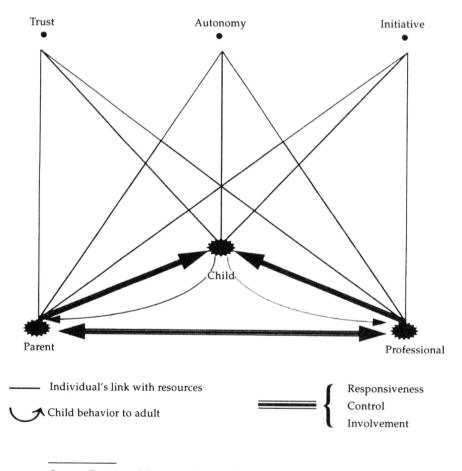

Source: Reprinted by permission, from M.B. Henry, *Young Children, Parents, and Professionals: Enhancing the Links in Early Childhood* (London: Routledge, 1996), 184.

Creating Communities for Learning

Conclusion

During a 12-week period, students are able to see the coherent picture of parent-teacher-child relationships emerging within the framework of the responsiveness/control/involvement dimensions. Even class meetings exemplify these dimensions when discussion allows a lively exchange of ideas. But it is in the field that a student like Jeanne becomes most aware of the needs and aims of parents and the resources teacher and parent gain from one another.

The teacher in training is able to offer her or his expertise to one parent and child and later to parents as a group. But equally, the teacher's own resources and those of the early childhood program are substantially enlarged because, like Paley (1995, 140), "she asked everyone to teach her." Teaching for reciprocal relationships rallies the resources of us all.

References

Amato, P. 1987. *Children in Australian families: The growth of competence.* Sydney: Prentice Hall.

Berger, E.H. 1995. *Parents as partners in education: Families and schools working together.* Englewood Cliffs, NJ: Prentice Hall.

Bredekamp, S., & C. Copple, eds. 1997. *Developmentally appropriate practice in early childhood programs.* Rev. ed. Washington DC: NAEYC.

Bronfenbrenner, U. 1969. Motivational and social components in compensatory education programs. In *Critical issues in research relating to disadvantaged children,* ed. E. Grotberg. Princeton, NJ: Educational Testing Service.

Chavkin, N.F. 1993. *Families and schools in a pluralistic society.* Albany: State University of New York Press.

Clarke-Stewart, K.A. 1987. Predicting child development from childcare forms and features: The Chicago study. In *Quality in child care: What does research tell us?* ed. D.A. Phillips. Washington, DC: NAEYC.

Croft, D. 1979. *Parents and teachers: A resource book for home, school, and community relations.* Belmont, CA: Wadsworth.

Davies, D. 1990. Shall we wait for the revolution? A few lessons from the Schools Reaching Out project. *Equity and Choice* 6 (3): 68–73.

de Acosta, M. 1996. A foundational approach to preparing teachers for family and community involvement in children's education. *Journal of Teacher Education* 47 (1): 9–15.

Epstein, J. 1992. School and family partnerships. In *Encyclopedia of educational research,* 1139–51. New York: Macmillan.

Erikson, E.H. 1950. *Childhood and society.* New York: Norton.

Gordon, I.J. 1972. What do we know about parents as teachers? *Theory into Practice* 11 (3): 146–49.

Gray, S.W., & R.A. Klaus. 1965. An experimental preschool program for culturally deprived children. *Child Development* 36 (4): 887–98.

Greenberg, P. 1989. Ideas that Work with Young Children. Parents as partners in young children's development and education. *Young Children* 44 (4): 61–75.

Greenwood, G., & C. Hickman. 1991. Research and practice in parent involvement: Implications for teacher education. *The Elementary School Journal* (91): 279–88.

Henry, M.B. 1992. An in-service program in family day care: Supporting the development of young children and their care providers. Ph.D. diss., University of Queensland, Brisbane, Australia.

Henry, M.B. 1996. *Young children, parents, and professionals: Enhancing the links in early childhood.* London: Routledge.

Hess, R.D. 1971. Community involvement in day care. *Day care: Resources for decisions.* Washington, DC: U.S. Office of Economic Opportunity.

James, T.E. 1975. *West Riding EPA project follow-up studies.* Oxford: Department of Social and Administrative Studies, Oxford University.

Larner, M. 1996. Parents' perspectives on quality in early care and education. In *Reinventing early care and education: A vision for a quality system,* eds. S. Kagan & N. Cohen, 21–42. San Francisco: Jossey-Bass.

Moles, O. 1993. Collaboration between schools and disadvantaged parents: Obstacles and openings. In *Families and schools in a pluralistic society,* ed. N.F. Chavkin, 21–49. Albany: State University of New York Press.

Murphy, D.M. 1997. Parent and teacher plan for the child. *Young Children* 52 (4): 32–36.

Ochiltree, G., & D. Edgar. 1995. *Today's child care, tomorrow's children!* Melbourne: Australian Institute of Family Studies.

Paley, V.G. 1995. *Kwanzaa and me.* Cambridge, MA: Harvard University Press.

Peters, D.L., & M.J. Kostelnik. 1981. Current research in day care personnel preparation. *Advances in Early Education and Day Care* (2): 29–60.

Powell, D.R. 1989. *Families and early childhood programs.* Washington, DC: NAEYC.

Powell, D.R. 1998. Research in Review. Reweaving parents into the fabric of early childhood programs. *Young Children* 53 (5): 60–67.

Raab, M., & C.J. Dunst. 1997. Early childhood program assessment scales and family support practices. In *Advances in early education and day care (Vol. 8): Family policy and practice in early education and child care programs,* series ed. S. Reifel, vol. eds. C.J. Dunst & M. Wolery, 105–31. Greenwich, CT: JAI.

Schaefer, E.S. 1968. Progress report: Intellectual stimulation of culturally deprived parents. Bethesda, MD: National Institute of Mental Health.

Stevenson, J., V, Bailey, & J. Simpson. 1988. Feasible intervention in families with parenting difficulties: A primary perspective on child abuse. In *Early prediction and prevention of child abuse,* eds. K. Browne, C. Davies, & P. Stratton. Chichester, UK: John Wiley.

Swap, S.M. 1991. How can we crack the "achievement barrier" in urban schools? *Equity and Choice* 7 (2 & 3): 58–64.

Williams, D., & N. Chavkin. 1987. *Teacher/parent partnerships: Guidelines and strategies to train elementary school teachers for parent involvement.* Austin, TX: Southwest Educational Development Laboratory.

Wolfendale, S. 1983. *Parental participation in children's development and education.* New York: Gordon & Breach.

Information about NAEYC

NAEYC is . . .

an organization of nearly 102,000 members, founded in 1926, that is committed to fostering the growth and development of children from birth through age 8. Membership is open to all who share a desire to serve young children and act on behalf of the needs and rights of all children.

NAEYC provides . . .

educational services and resources to adults and programs working with and for children, including

• *Young Children, the* peer-reviewed journal for early childhood educators

• **Books, posters, brochures, position statements, and videos** to expand your knowledge and commitment and support your work with young children and families, including such topics as inclusion, diversity, literacy, guidance, assessment, developmentally appropriate practice, and teaching

• **An Annual Conference,** the largest education conference in North America, that brings people together from across the United States and other countries to share their expertise and advocate on behalf of children and families

• **Week of the Young Child** celebrations planned annually by NAEYC Affiliate Groups in communities around the country to call public attention to the critical significance of the child's early years

• **Insurance plans** for members and programs

• **Public affairs information,** and access to information through NAEYC resources and communication systems, for conducting knowledgeable advocacy efforts at all levels of government and in the media

• **A voluntary accreditation system** for high-quality programs for children through the National Academy of Early Childhood Programs

• **Professional development resources and programs** through the National Institute for Early Childhood Professional Development, working to improve the quality and consistency of early childhood preparation and leadership opportunities

• **Young Children International** to promote international communication, discussion forums, and information exchanges

For information about membership, publications, or other NAEYC services, visit NAEYC online at **www.naeyc.org**

National Association for the Education of Young Children
1509 16th Street, NW, Washington, DC 20036-1426
202-232-8777 or 800-424-2460